MEDICINE
FOR
SALE

THE GRAND ROUNDS PRESS

MEDICINE FOR SALE

RICHARD CURREY

WHITTLE DIRECT BOOKS

THE GRAND ROUNDS PRESS

The Grand Rounds Press presents original short books by distinguished authors on subjects of importance to the medical profession.

The series is edited and published by Whittle Books, a business unit of Whittle Communications L.P. A new book is published approximately every three months. The series reflects a broad spectrum of responsible opinions. In each book the opinions expressed are those of the author, not the publisher or advertiser.

I welcome your comments on this unique endeavor.

William S. Rukeyser
Editor in Chief

For
Leon S. Gottlieb, M.D.,
teacher, mentor, longtime friend

Photographs: John Wesley Powell: the Bettmann Archive, page 6; Sidney Garfield: courtesy of the Bancroft Library, University of California at Berkeley, page 8; Grand Coulee Dam: Culver Pictures Inc., page 9; Morris Fishbein and Henry Kaiser: AP/Wide World Photos, page 15; Thomas Percival: courtesy of the New York Academy of Medicine, page 22; Editorial cartoon: reprinted by permission of Tribune Media Services, page 24; Ernest Barnes by Tim Redel, page 26; Vern Miller: *Topeka Capital-Journal*, page 30; Barry Costilo and Newton Minow: AP/Wide World Photos, page 34; Michael Halberstam: courtesy of New York Academy of Medicine, page 36; Robert Ebert: courtesy of the National Library of Medicine, Washington, D.C., page 37; Ron Wyden: AP/Wide World Photos, page 46; Fortney Stark: the Bettmann Archive, page 48; Arnold Relman by Larry Maglott, page 51; Raymond Gavery by Leonard Freed/Magnum Photos Inc., page 56; Armand Gonzalzles by Leonard Freed/Magnum Photos Inc., page 60; Thomas Krizek by Paul Elledge, page 68.

Library of Congress Catalog Card Number: 91-67094
Currey, Richard
Medicine For Sale
ISBN 1-879736-04-7
ISSN 1053-6620

*"It is no disparagement of honorable trades and callings . . .
to insist that an organized profession of physicians
is not primarily analogous to a retail
grocers' association . . . that there is a generic distinction
between a medical society and a plumbers' or
lumber dealers' association. It is unhappily true that there
was in the last century in America a tendency to
deprofessionalize the old professions, to reduce all callings to
the level of individual business enterprise, and to think of
medical societies or bar associations as like trade
organizations. But the root purpose is different. The trade
association exists for the purposes of money-making activity.
The medical society exists primarily for the purposes of
medicine, for the advancement of the healing art."*

— **ROSCOE POUND**
Dean of Harvard Law School, 1916-1936
from "The Professions in the Society of Today"
in *The New England Journal of Medicine,*
September 8, 1949

CONTENTS

PREFACE

he commercialization of American health care—
a process that has helped to change medicine from
a loose collective of individual practitioners to a
gargantuan industry—has altered the heart of
modern medical practice. Like it or not, today's physicians
must cope with the idea of medicine as a marketable product,
an arena of still-untapped retail potential. Everywhere now,
doctors are seen as entrepreneurs as well as caregivers, business people whose particular service just happens to be the
practice of medicine. There are franchised "care units," medical service "outlets," medical-practice consultants, medical
credit cards, physician-owned pharmacies and diagnostic centers, even physicians with personal press agents.

The most pervasive expression of this rapidly proliferating
commercialization is advertising. It is no longer peculiar or,
more important, unethical for physicians to aggressively use
any and all marketing methods available to promote themselves. Medical care is now advertised in every medium, using
sophisticated techniques and professionally managed ad cam-
paigns. The 1980s brought full-page advertisements for physicians in newspapers, intimate *Marcus Welby*-style television
spots, and ads on the sides of city buses in places like New York,
Chicago, and Los Angeles.

The immediate and obvious question inspired by this state
of affairs is one of balance and value: has rampant commercialization weakened medicine's longstanding and closely held
traditions to the detriment of patients as well as society at large?

There are those who dismiss such concerns as antiquated
and rooted in what they see as medicine's grandiose sense of

1

self-importance. To allow doctors to compete in the commercial mainstream, they maintain, is to allow normal market forces to prevail—no more, no less. Competition, after all, is an American ideal that should lead to the best service at the lowest price.

Others believe that commercialism has undermined what were always the finest features of American medicine, trivializing an already beleaguered profession while doing little to improve services and lower prices.

Between these two camps this much is certain: the nature of medical practice and of the physician's professional identity is undergoing its most basic conceptual shift since the advent of technological medicine in the 1950s. In the balance are concerns much more crucial than simply the ethics of advertising. Though the mores of marketing might tend to draw doctors into conflicts of interest or tempt them to blur the edges of accuracy in their promotional messages, such problems are only the iceberg's tip. For the first time since the profession's inception, clinicians find themselves contending with practices burdened by federal regulation, with prices wildly inflated by the cost of technology and patient care—all of it complicated by a revisionist view of health care as a range of consumer goods, to be marketed and sold as such.

In spite of serious obstruction by medicine's old guard—largely originating from the American Medical Association and its *Principles of Medical Ethics,* which sharply curtailed any sort of competitive business behavior among doctors—medicine's current embrace of business principles would almost certainly have evolved under the influence of ever-growing competition for a share of dwindling health-care dollars. Sparked by the rise of prepaid health plans, questions of medical commercialism and professional ethics were argued passionately in the 30 years after World War II in a host of AMA judicial opinions, sanctions, and censures. In 1975 the Federal Trade Commission carried the argument into the courts when it took on the AMA over the same issues.

Medicine-as-a-business received the formal imprimatur of the Supreme Court in 1982, when the Court found in favor of the FTC. Easily one of the most significant events in the his-

"I am on the verge of mysteries and the veil is getting thinner and thinner."

Miles is proud to present this series on...

Powerful Innovators

Powerful Innovator

Louis Pasteur (1822-1895)

Even on the morning of his wedding, Pasteur had to be torn away from his laboratory experiments for the ceremony.

Accomplished in biology and chemistry, Pasteur was the first scientist to prove that heating a beverage to kill unwanted microbes would not ruin it—a fear of vintners who were looking for ways to keep their wine from souring with age. Although milk is pasteurized today, Pasteur originally used his methods on wine and beer.

Pasteur's most impressive achievement was his contribution to the germ theory of disease. He spent much time lecturing on the importance of stopping or limiting the spread of bacterial disease through changes in hospital practices.

Pasteur also founded the science of immunization and introduced the word "vaccine" to scientific language. His development of a rabies vaccine earned him worldwide fame and honor as well as funding for his new Institute.

Powerful Antimicrobial

Another reason the power of Cipro® stands out is its unique mode of action. It lets the power of Cipro® remain unaffected by ß-lactamase or plasmid-mediated resistance. And cross-resistance, which often limits the usefulness of other classes of antibiotics, is not a problem reported with Cipro®. In fact, Cipro® kills susceptible pathogens* during the four phases of cell growth.† Another advantage you do not get with other antiinfectives.

Cipro® TABLETS

(ciprofloxacin HCl)

The most potent fluoroquinolone. [1-3‡]

* Due to susceptible strains of indicated pathogens. See indicated organisms in prescribing information.
† Data on file, Miles Inc Pharmaceutical Division.
‡ In vitro activity does not necessarily imply a correlation with in vivo results.
§ Estimate based on prescription data from IMS, *National Prescription Audit*, and PDS, *U.S. Hospital Drug and Diagnosis Audit*, October 1987 through June 1990.

See full prescribing information at the end of this book.

Powerful Numbers

Speak for themselves

*1 ...The number of **fluoroquinolones** indicated for lower respiratory infections, skin and skin structure infections, bone and joint infections, urinary tract infections, infectious diarrhea.**

96 ...The percentage of favorable clinical response (resolution + improvement) with Cipro® in lower respiratory infections due to susceptible strains of indicated pathogens.

13,000,000...The estimated number of patients treated to date with Cipro® in this country.§

Cipro® TABLETS

(ciprofloxacin HCl)

The most potent fluoroquinolone.[1-3‡]

CIPRO® SHOULD NOT BE USED IN CHILDREN, ADOLESCENTS, OR PREGNANT WOMEN.

See full prescribing information at the end of this book.

COMMITTED TO THERAPEUTIC EFFICIENCY

MILES

Miles Inc.
Pharmaceutical Division
400 Morgan Lane
West Haven, CT 06516

© March 1991, Miles Inc. Pharmaceutical Division   Printed in U.S.A.   CO957G tory of medicine, the Supreme Court's 4-4 split upheld the lower courts: the American Medical Association had conspired with its local affiliate societies to unlawfully restrain competition among physicians. The AMA was ordered to cease and desist. Physicians were, in effect, given permission to sell their skills in any legitimate manner they saw fit. It was the gateway to a new kind of medicine—the medicine of franchises, telemarketing, direct mail, and celebrity doctors. The medicine of the 21st century.

CHAPTER ONE

KAISER WAKES THE DOCTORS

During most of this country's history, the concerns of business were held to be beyond the purview of the physician. Before 1940, the practice of medicine was largely an art, the province of the gifted counselor and the humanitarian. In an America where there were never too many doctors or too few patients, physicians merely hung a shingle, and the patients came. The profession held to a set of time-honored ethical beliefs organized around altruism, beneficence, and community spirit; notions of openly competing with other doctors or directly soliciting patients were clearly unacceptable.

The fee-for-service solo practitioner—the country doctor— was an American archetype. Although technology had not yet provided physicians with the array of tools they have today, the services doctors offered squarely met the needs of their communities. People had the care they wanted, at a price they could afford.

That state of affairs would be changed forever by the arrival of the prepaid health plan, a system that seemed on the surface to violate medicine's traditional prohibitions against the solicitation of patients and contract practice. The events that would set this process in motion came with the evolution of another growth industry in the years just before World War II: the irrigation of the arid Western states.

The idea of bringing water to the West—of creating arable land out of basin and desert—began with a quintessential

Western hero, John Wesley Powell. A decorated artillery officer in the Civil War, a legendary explorer, naturalist, and anthropologist, Powell served as director of the United States Geological Survey from 1881 to 1892. In that capacity he brought a revolutionary idea before Congress: the vast country west of the Mississippi could be reclaimed for agriculture, he asserted, using the water from a carefully designed system of dams and reservoirs to irrigate the plains. While scientifically sound, Powell's ideas involved approaches too utilitarian and communal to suit the expansionist mood of the country and its politicians in the late 19th century. He would not live to see his vision of a multimillion-dollar federal irrigation project put into practice.

Fifty years after Powell's proposal to Congress, drought had turned the yeoman farmers of the Southwest into a generation of homeless migrants, devastated by poverty and the destruction of an entire way of life. The once untenable notions of John Wesley Powell gained new currency. The country was no longer big enough, and Powell's idea for "redeeming" the West was clearly the only way to go. So began what Marc Reisner, in *Cadillac Desert*, his elegant study of Western water, calls "a half-century rampage of dam-building and irrigation development." No one could have foreseen that this great push toward an irrigated West would sound the death knell for the beloved country doctor and change the face of American medicine.

The first big Western river that had to be "tamed" was the Colorado. Rising in the Rockies in northwestern Colorado, it collects the waters of 50 feeder streams on a 1,400-mile route across Colorado, Utah, Arizona, and Nevada, forms the border between Arizona and California, and empties into the Gulf of California. A major dam on the Colorado had been under discussion since the turn of the century for one good reason: the continuing development of the Imperial Valley in California and the growth of the city of Los Angeles.

The water demands of Imperial Valley agriculture and metropolitan Los Angeles were already overwhelming by 1930; the nearest likely source was the Colorado River. But no dam of such scope or sheer size had ever been attempted in human

Explorer and geologist John Wesley Powell (far left) was the first to propose the irrigation of the West. His companions in this 1875 studio photograph are unidentified.

history. No single engineering firm existed at the time that could take on such a project. It took, literally, an act of Congress to put into motion both the massive funding and extraordinary engineering creativity needed to build a dam across the Colorado.

The site selected was a desert canyon about 30 miles from Las Vegas, Nevada. The Department of the Interior called for bids on what was known as the Boulder Canyon Project. There were, of course, no rules for such an undertaking, no blueprints, nobody with experience. Among others, two Western contractors were drawn to the notion of building this engineering wonder. One was an aging road builder named W. A. Bechtel. The other was an up-and-coming contractor named Henry J. Kaiser. With six other engineering firms, Bechtel and Kaiser organized a first-of-its-kind conglomerate called Six

Companies, incorporating in February of 1931, barely two weeks before formal bidding opened on the Boulder Canyon Project.

There were only two other serious competitors for the job, both of which were two-company consortiums. Six Companies Inc. came in with the lowest bid—just under $49 million—and work began on the dam on March 11, 1931.

Kaiser—who got his start in general construction in 1914 and went on to become one of the greatest industrialists of the West, founding Kaiser Steel and Kaiser Aluminum and Chemical Company—supervised the construction of the dam from his corporate offices in Oakland, California. At the work site in the Nevada desert, the workers' daily round of dynamiting and rock slides was followed by evenings in "Ragtown," an adjacent squatters' camp. The only amenity was the river itself, shared for drinking, cooking, washing, and waste. Local health officials decried the primitive conditions, citing a high risk of epidemic diseases among Six Companies workers and the other inhabitants of Ragtown.

Kaiser, then 49 years old, knew something about country doctors and medical care: he had been involved in securing health-care coverage for his gravel and paving workers on rural road projects in the Pacific Northwest during World War I. He knew the monetary value of keeping his employees healthy. This perspective was shared by his longtime associate Alonzo Ordway, director of Industrial Indemnity, the company that insured the dam workers. (Industrial Indemnity was partially owned by Six Companies.)

Kaiser and Ordway first attempted to improve their workers' health status by building Boulder City, a community of barracks, two- and three-room houses, and a mess hall. But it wasn't until 1933 that Ordway heard about a young physician who was working as a company doctor for the Colorado River Aqueduct Project (separate from the Boulder Dam project but also insured by Industrial Indemnity) some 120 miles southwest of Boulder Canyon.

Dr. Sidney R. Garfield had gone into the desert from Los Angeles to serve as a company doctor for the builders of the Colorado River Aqueduct, the pipeline that would carry the

Colorado's water to Los Angeles. With the Depression in full swing, Garfield found that even the medical profession was affected by declines in both opportunity and available money. His solution was to take on what he assumed would be a temporary assignment in contract practice in the small town of Desert Center, California, midway along the aqueduct's route.

In the early 1930s, the concept of a prepaid health plan for a company's employees was hardly new. Railroad and lumber concerns had funded such systems as early as the Civil War years, and some coal operators had tried the idea in the 1880s. Although these early forms of contract medicine represented progressive thinking, they held few real incentives for physicians. When Garfield went to Desert Center, his clinic was an out-of-pocket gamble: the construction company's insurer would pay his claims, but there was little additional financial support. Most of the medicine Garfield delivered was one-shot emergency care—not the sort of work that builds a practice. Within months, Garfield was nearing personal bankruptcy. He was unable to meet a minimal payroll, and his creditors loomed.

At that point, prepaid health care for industrial workers seemed the only way to go. When Alonzo Ordway learned of Garfield's dilemma, he recognized that allowing the doctor to return to Los Angeles was not in the best interest of Six Companies or its employees. Although Garfield's distance from Boulder Canyon meant that he could have little immediate impact on the dam project, Ordway knew a good investment when he saw one. In an act of remarkable managerial foresight, he offered to mediate negotiations to save Garfield's contract practice.

Under the new agreement, Garfield would provide nonindustrial and nonemergency health care in addition to emergency care to the aqueduct's 5,000 workers. Garfield aimed to deliver the finest medical care possible under the circumstances. He offered preventive medicine and safety counseling, realizing they would save lives and money, although these areas of health care would not become fashionable in fee-for-service medical practice for another 40 years.

After the aqueduct was completed in 1938, Garfield packed his bags. His job was over, he thought. He had no idea that he

A 1942 photo of Dr. Sidney Garfield, whose vision of a prepaid health plan for workers became the Kaiser-Permanente Medical Care Program

Garfield and Associates provided prepaid health care from 1938 until 1942 for 5,000 workers at Grand Coulee Dam. This is a scene from the construction site in Washington State.

would return again to prepaid health care, or that his name would be linked to a formidable new movement in American medicine.

Boulder Dam (renamed Hoover Dam in 1931) was a legitimate engineering marvel. Kaiser's Six Companies had done what many held to be impossible, and the corporation was hungry to try again. The opportunity came two years later. The next great dam was another "impossibility": the Grand Coulee across the Columbia River.

The Columbia was the biggest river that anyone had ever considered damming. Flowing south out of British Columbia into Washington State, the Columbia dwarfs the Colorado in terms of water volume and descent. It drains an area twice the size of Great Britain. Building the dam at Grand Coulee in a remote section of eastern Washington State in the mid-1930s presented an entirely new set of engineering problems, one of which was simply controlling the Columbia's thundering waters to allow construction. The project would be another massive affair involving thousands of workers and several years on a wild and dangerous site.

This time Ordway was ready, recommending Sidney Garfield to Edgar Kaiser (Henry's 30-year-old son, who was supervising the project) as the man to organize high-quality on-site medical services. Assured of more comfortable corporate support for his work than in his earlier experiment with contract practice, Garfield agreed to work at Grand Coulee under a prepaid employee health plan.

Garfield and Associates became the medical contractor to Six Companies in 1938. Garfield hired six other doctors and a large support staff to deal with some 5,000 workers. With the backing of the company and labor unions, he expanded his focus and soon provided a full range of medical services to workers' families as well. Eventually, he also provided fee-for-service care to visiting bureaucrats, local business people—anyone in the area who needed medical attention. The quality of care was consistently first-rate and, again, Garfield's project was deemed a success. The first broad-based health maintenance organization in American history was born.

The effectiveness of prepaid health care was not lost on Henry Kaiser and his executives. Kaiser saw several attractive options in the idea of affordable health care for the working man, not the least of which was an ability to save money for his companies and keep lost man-hours to a minimum. Before the Grand Coulee was completed in 1942, Kaiser had turned his attention to wartime shipbuilding. Garfield went along.

Kaiser's shipyards became vital to the war effort, and it was in this environment that Garfield and Associates went even further with its prepaid health plan. Garfield set up a field hospital for shipyard emergencies, established ambulance units, and convinced Kaiser to guarantee a loan to rebuild an Oakland hospital that would serve as an "in-house" facility for health-plan members. By 1944 there were 200,000 subscribers to what would come to be known as the Kaiser-Permanente Medical Care Program ("Permanente" was the name of a creek in Southern California that Kaiser loved), with hospitals in San Francisco and Portland, Oregon.

Helping things along for the Kaiser-Permanente Medical Care Program was an energetic freelance journalist named Paul de Kruif. A popular medical writer of the time, de Kruif discovered Kaiser and Garfield's new health-care system as the Grand Coulee was being completed, and he became an enthusiastic convert to what he decided would be the salvation of American medicine. Although he was aware that prepaid industrial health-care programs were not new, de Kruif was convinced that Sidney Garfield's systematic upgrades in prepaid care represented the best and brightest version of the idea ever—the "Mayo Clinic of the common man." De Kruif interviewed Kaiser and wrote an admiring article for the May 1943 issue of *Reader's Digest* called "Tomorrow's Health Plan—Today!"

Later in the same year de Kruif published a book entitled *Kaiser Wakes the Doctors*, a flamboyant account of the rise of the Kaiser health plan. The general tone of this slim volume was that of a promotional pamphlet, with de Kruif's zeal reaching nearly religious intensity as he touted "efforts to bring maximum medical care within the reach of all people" and described Henry Kaiser's "medical mercy" and "epic generosity."

Midway through *Kaiser Wakes the Doctors*, de Kruif interrupted his story to discuss a situation he feared could become a problem for the Kaiser-Permanente program. He related the particulars of a 1938 case in Washington, D.C., in which the District of Columbia Medical Society had boycotted physicians working in a prepaid-medical-care program called the Group Health Association. The society charged that in working for an organization that actively sought patient-members, these physicians were violating the AMA's ethical tenets against patient solicitation. The society vigorously threatened the doctors with expulsion from both the local society and the AMA, an action that could have endangered their hospital privileges. Responding to complaints by the Group Health Association, the Justice Department indicted 21 doctors—presiding officials at the D.C. Medical Society and at the AMA—for "restraint of trade."

In keeping with his hyperbolic style, de Kruif described the case as "looking like Armageddon," and suggested this same fight would come to Kaiser-Permanente in California. De Kruif, in essence, dismissed the AMA's position as not in keeping with such higher values as truth, justice, and the welfare of the common man, and predicted eventual victory for his heroes, Dr. Sidney Garfield and Henry J. Kaiser. Despite his florid style, de Kruif was prescient about the extent and passion of the dispute over physician ethics and patient solicitation, both as a stumbling block to projects like Kaiser's and as the first stage in the larger battle for control of medical care in the United States. De Kruif called *D.C. Medical Society* v. *Group Health Association* a "test case for the nation." Meanwhile, other such test cases were shaping up by the end of World War II—cases that would lead directly to the Federal Trade Commission's suit against the American Medical Association in 1975.

CHAPTER TWO

THE BATTLE BEGINS

s World War II neared an end, a loose collective of Seattle's union locals founded its own medical co-operative, working with payments of $100 solicited from each of 400 contributing families. The Group Health Cooperative of Puget Sound immediately encountered opposition from Seattle's medical community. In 1945, the King County Medical Society found the cooperative's "solicitation" of a patient base to be contradictory to the generally accepted behavior of physicians, and in violation of the AMA's *Principles of Medical Ethics.* We can also assume that society members didn't like the idea of losing income to the co-op: they created opposition at every turn, denying co-op physicians hospital privileges, access to continuing education, and membership in the society.

Still, for its working-class members with no other medical alternatives, the Group Health Cooperative of Puget Sound was a godsend.

Meanwhile, Sidney Garfield was encountering problems with the medical societies in San Francisco. Bay Area physicians were no more pleased with the Kaiser plan than their Seattle colleagues were with Group Health. Such "closed panel systems" (as they were then called) went against the grain of American medicine's sense of itself as a healing art rendered solely by individuals in private practice.

Medicine, by tradition, was not a "business" in any formal sense, and it was certainly not a corporate enterprise. So one issue was simply that of longstanding, genteel custom. Then, obviously, there was the more painful issue of private physicians' loss of revenue to the closed-panel systems. But it was wartime, and Garfield's innovative organization, which provided health care for workers engaged in shipbuilding, was squarely in the center of the war effort. That was a major factor in precluding complaints from individual doctors or affiliate societies of the AMA until 1945.

When the war was over, Sidney Garfield and Henry Kaiser made what must have seemed an obvious decision at the time. Given the growth and effectiveness of Kaiser-Permanente, they decided to sell the plan's services to the general public. Kaiser, ever mindful of his humanitarian image—and clearly a man with a refined nose for money—saw a superb combination of financial and self-promotion opportunities in the health plan. In a letter from the period, Kaiser talked about the "rapid development of this new type of medical service which would surpass anything thus far developed in the United States or any other country."

The American Medical Association had other ideas. The problems entailed in building immense dams in the middle of nowhere had created a peculiar, unexpected side effect: a huge, established medical "agency," ready to dispense everything a patient might need. The basic issue was clearly competition, though it ran counter to the AMA's dignified traditions to approach the matter directly.

The first criticism of Garfield and of Kaiser-Permanente had actually been vented during the war. During congressional testimony in 1942, Dr. Morris Fishbein (then editor of *The Journal of the American Medical Association*) claimed that Garfield had undermined the war effort by recruiting physicians who should have been on active duty at the front lines. In the larger framework of the war it was a trivial complaint, easily dismissed given the range of Garfield's work and the importance of Kaiser's shipyards. And Fishbein's credibility was already eroding: an elderly man considered too conservative even for the AMA, he was, in fact, fired as *JAMA*'s editor seven years later due to continual accusations of unethical practices. But though Fishbein was silenced, his hostility was a harbinger of things to come.

The AMA's Morris Fishbein (right), editor of _JAMA_, assailed the Garfield-Kaiser prepaid health system before Congress in 1942, as an angry Henry J. Kaiser (left) looked on.

Although Kaiser-Permanente's membership fell after the war, organized labor supported the prepaid-health-plan concept because it had improved the lives and health of union members during the war years. This endorsement was fundamental in saving the health plan and setting the stage for its expansion. But while this was happening, Garfield found himself under constant fire from the local AMA affiliate, the California Medical Board (CMB).

As far as the AMA was concerned, Kaiser-Permanente was showing ominous signs of survival and, worse, growth. Something needed to be done to preserve not only an equitable marketplace, but also the overriding dignity of the profession. The obvious target was Dr. Sidney Garfield; the weapon would be a charge of medical malfeasance, leveled in 1946.

Garfield's alleged violation was the employment of an un-licensed physician. Lieutenant Colonel Clifford Keene, fresh-ly returned from Army service as a combat surgeon, was interviewed by Garfield for employment in the Kaiser-Per-manente system on January 3, 1946. Still in uniform at his in-terview, Keene reminded Garfield that he did not yet have his California license. Given Keene's military service (he'd had several field commands and chief-of-surgery posts in military hospitals) and his auspicious background as chief surgical res-ident at the University of Michigan before the war, Garfield as-sumed the wait for licensure would present no problem. To sidestep the licensure requirement, Garfield suggested that Keene be temporarily designated a resident and start work at the Permanente Hospital in Oakland.

In 1946, as the California Medical Board was seeking to bring down Garfield and the Kaiser system, Keene's employ-ment was just the infraction it was looking for. After a brief hearing, Garfield was placed on five years' probation, and his license to practice medicine was suspended. He appealed in court and saw the decision reversed. Meanwhile, Keene re-ceived his California license in June 1946, which rendered the case moot.

Having weathered this assault, Garfield was subsequently charged with soliciting patients, a specific violation of profes-sional ethics. These new charges came from the Alameda Med-ical Association, from which the physician was suspended in 1948.

These sorts of maneuvers (or close variations) would come to be the stock-in-trade enforcement techniques of the AMA's local affiliate societies, as resistance to a more commercialized and product-oriented medicine moved into the 1950s. Garfield and Associates and Kaiser-Permanente continued to grow and diversify during this period, and they frequently had to defend their position against the AMA's attacks. A public statement by the Los Angeles County Medical Association in 1953 declared such systems as Garfield's "to be undesirable and injurious to the public" and stated that doctors who worked for him, or for any closed-panel system, were not act-ing within "the letter or the spirit of the *Principles of Medical*

Ethics of the American Medical Association." In Seattle, the King County Medical Society continued to boycott the Group Health Cooperative until 1951. The treatment of the entire controversy—in both the popular and professional media—was laden with the metaphors of combat.

The battle between fee-for-service practitioners and closed panels was basically a battle for dollars. The terms of the argument have never changed, even as the conflict that began before World War II has grown immeasurably more complex. At the center of this often bitter history, however, is an honorable concern—medicine's sense of itself as a worthy endeavor in human affairs, an undertaking built on a prevailing sense of duty and caring.

A war for livelihood coupled with a war for basic values—such are the makings of the proverbial Good Fight. A cause that involves beliefs that are literally and figuratively worth fighting for cannot be easily dismissed. This undoubtedly energized the solo practitioners of the West Coast in their fierce encounters with Garfield and the Group Health Cooperative in Seattle. The seeds of defeat, however, were sown early.

The first setback for organized medicine came in 1942, when the District of Columbia Medical Society and the AMA were found guilty of restraint of trade in the *Group Health Association* case. And in 1951, the Washington State Supreme Court ordered the King County Medical Society to drop its six-year boycott of the Group Health Cooperative of Puget Sound. Then, in 1953, came a critical and hard-fought engagement in Northern California.

In the summer of that year, a group of private physicians in Pittsburg, California, took to the streets with their wives, sound trucks, and thousands of leaflets ("Support Your Family Doctor!") in an attempt to block yet another incursion by Kaiser and Garfield.

Kaiser-Permanente had just opened a hospital in Walnut Creek, 15 miles east of Oakland. It planned to do the same in Pittsburg, just a few miles north of Walnut Creek and about the same distance to the east of the Oakland-San Francisco metropolitan area. As it happened, Pittsburg was the seat of Columbia Steel, which had thousands of plant workers—all potential members of Kaiser-Permanente. It was the kind of setup that Garfield and Kaiser had cut their teeth on, and in fact, negotiations between the steelworkers' local and Kaiser-Permanente were under way before the formal announcement of Kaiser's entry into Pittsburg was made in June 1953.

But the small city on Suisun Bay also had 30 private physicians already in place, enjoying practices built to a large degree on the patronage of steelworkers and their families. The doctors of Pittsburg were determined to fight.

Henry Kaiser asserted that medical service was a product like anything else, and that consumers should be allowed to decide what they wanted. When Local 1440 of the United Steelworkers of America declared itself in favor of the Kaiser plan, the physicians of Pittsburg asked that the decision be put to a workers' vote.

The referendum was held on Labor Day 1953, and the doctors of Pittsburg took their fight to the sidewalks, parking lots, and storefronts of the town they served. The physicians campaigned with newspaper ads, billboards, and radio announcements. Sound trucks trolled through the streets telling the citizens of Pittsburg, "Retain your family doctor!" There was heavy leafleting at the plant gates; the idea of air-dropping leaflets was considered. Kaiser's people responded in kind; union leaders promoted the intrinsic merits of the Kaiser plan to their members.

Given its later opposition to advertising, it is noteworthy that the AMA did not seem to have problems with the aggressive advertising techniques used by the Pittsburg doctors in their attempt to chase Kaiser out of town. As it happened, these techniques failed. At day's end the results of the balloting were conclusive. The workers of Columbia Steel selected Kaiser-Permanente as their health-care provider by a ratio of nearly 5 to 1.

But things did not get much easier for Kaiser-Permanente after the defeat of the Pittsburg doctors. It was only one month later, in October 1953, that Paul de Kruif, longtime supporter and ardent publicist of the health plan, defected to the enemy. In a "confession of personal error" originally published in the *Bulletin of the Los Angeles County Medical Association*, and

His experience as a World War I army doctor treating battle wounds with antiseptics helped set his goal to develop agents that would eradicate microbes without hurting normal body tissue...

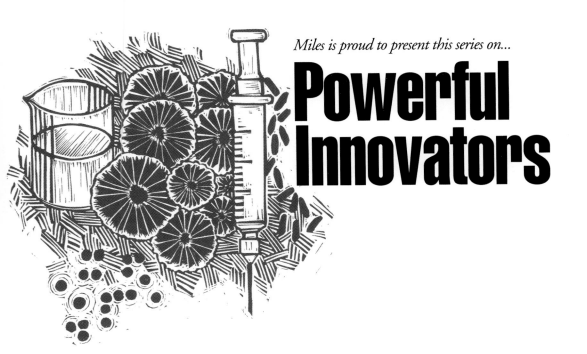

Miles is proud to present this series on...

Powerful Innovators

Powerful Physician

Sir Alexander Fleming (1881-1955)

Sir Alexander Fleming made history by successfully strengthening our hand in the struggle for survival and the way we treat infectious diseases.

His "chance observation" in 1928 that the mold <u>Penicillium</u> <u>notatum</u> inhibited the growth of a culture plate of staphylococci was reported clearly and concisely to the medical community in a mere 12 pages.

It took 12 years before Drs. Florey and Chain solicited and received the help of America's pharmaceutical manufacturers, followed shortly thereafter by aid from the American government. (This made the production of penicillin a top priority; ultimately, it shared federal funds with atomic bomb development.)

World War II effectively established the value of penicillin and Fleming's remarkable achievement, earning him the 1945 Nobel Prize in medicine and physiology.

Powerful Antimicrobial

Making history every day as the most potent fluoroquinolone, Cipro® gives today's physician excellent antimicrobial activity against many gram-negative and gram-positive pathogens, with impressive tissue penetration and serum concentration.† Every day, Cipro® gives physicians the power to eradicate tough infections while giving patients the freedom to resume their lives.*

Cipro® TABLETS

(ciprofloxacin HCl)

The most potent fluoroquinolone. [1-3‡]

* Due to susceptible strains of indicated pathogens. See indicated organisms in prescribing information.
† Tissue/fluid penetration is regarded as essential to therapeutic efficacy, but penetration levels have not been correlated with specific therapeutic results.
‡ In vitro activity does not necessarily imply a correlation with in vivo results.
§ Projected from U.S. data.

See full prescribing information at the end of this book.

Powerful Numbers

Speak for themselves

*1 ...The number of **fluoroquinolones** indicated for lower respiratory infections, skin and skin structure infections, bone and joint infections, urinary tract infections, infectious diarrhea.**

12 ...Number of hours serum concentrations of Cipro® are maintained in excess of $MIC_{90}s$ of most susceptible bacteria.†

22,030,000 ...The estimated number of patients treated with Cipro® worldwide.§

Cipro® TABLETS
(ciprofloxacin HCl)

The most potent fluoroquinolone. [1-3‡]

CIPRO® SHOULD NOT BE USED IN CHILDREN, ADOLESCENTS, OR PREGNANT WOMEN.

See full prescribing information at the end of this book.

COMMITTED TO THERAPEUTIC EFFICIENCY

MILES

Miles Inc.
Pharmaceutical Division
400 Morgan Lane
West Haven, CT 06516

© March 1991, Miles Inc. Pharmaceutical Division   Printed in U.S.A.   CO9570F later in *Medical Economics*, de Kruif claimed that his lavish praise for the Kaiser-Garfield ideal had been precipitate. Everything had seemed wonderful at Grand Coulee during the desperate moments of World War II—but now, in the clear light of a thriving postwar America, de Kruif claimed he had been misled. Garfield and Kaiser, he had come to believe, were merely a pair of self-interested fortune hunters. Their avowed commitment to truly accessible and affordable national health care was little more than corporate propaganda.

Wherever the truth of the matter lay, it seems clear that de Kruif recanted because of a personal disappointment. He had hoped to secure positions for some friends of his—medical research scientists—at Kaiser-Permanente. Garfield chose not to hire de Kruif's friends, which led the author to claim that Kaiser-Permanente had suffered "failures in the research area." After this, de Kruif began to find other failings in the Kaiser-Permanente system, and he pressed Garfield to declare a truce with fee-for-service practitioners and to become an "open panel," that is, to honor insurance claims from out-of-plan physicians. Henry Kaiser wouldn't hear of it.

At that point, de Kruif decided that Kaiser was no longer a hero. Dr. Sidney Garfield had fallen from near sainthood and become a cold, flat character who "no longer believed in human relationships" in the practice of medicine. Perhaps, de Kruif asserted, the AMA had been right all along: closed-panel medicine was unethical and failed to deliver on its promise of the best care for everybody. By the middle of 1953, he concluded that neither Kaiser nor Garfield "had any real intention of seeking peaceful relations with private-practice medicine," and he announced that his hopes for the Kaiser health-care plan were dead. "Such has been my mistake," de Kruif wrote, "and for that I can only admit: *mea culpa.*"

De Kruif's defection was no small matter, given his status with the American public. He published widely in the most popular magazines of the day, and his books sold well. His was a respected voice. If Paul de Kruif said something, it must surely be so. But Garfield and Kaiser had become accustomed to persisting against a constant tide of criticism, and despite de Kruif's "confession," Kaiser-Permanente's foot was in the door.

The concept born of Sidney Garfield's health-care system for dam workers in the Depression would come to every part of California within the next two decades.

Still, concerns about what many doctors saw as a damaging abuse of medical professionalism continued to simmer.

CHAPTER THREE

A QUESTION OF PROFESSIONALISM

he AMA's *Principles of Medical Ethics* had been leveled against Kaiser and Garfield more as a weapon than as a set of professional tenets. This same document would directly link Garfield's troubles in the late 1940s to the Federal Trade Commission's case against the AMA some 30 years later.

Physicians' codes of conduct go back thousands of years, to Hammurabi (2500 B.C.) and Hippocrates (500 B.C.). These earliest canons were far more concerned with appropriate social behavior than matters of commerce. Hippocrates, for example, cautioned physicians against casting an appreciative eye toward a patient's wife or daughter. As to business, he encouraged decorum in discussing such sordid matters as fees. "For should you begin by discussing fees," he wrote in his *Precepts,* "you will suggest to the patient either that you will go away and leave him if no agreement be reached, or that you will neglect him and not prescribe any immediate treatment. So one must not be anxious about setting a fee."

By the 18th century, however, some English physicians were more clearly acknowledging the existence of business concerns. In his *Discourse Upon the Duties of a Physician* (circa 1769), Dr. Samuel Bard counseled, "Let your integrity be proof against the temptation of unnecessarily multiplying prescriptions . . . for although you may sometimes think your services undervalued, yet you will always enjoy the superior satisfaction of conscious rectitude. . . . "

The AMA's *Principles,* adopted at the organization's first convention in Philadelphia in 1847, draws heavily from Dr. Thomas Percival's *Code of Medical Ethics* (1803). Percival's small book is remarkable, a pocket compendium of medical philosophy that remains very liberal and "holistic" by today's standards. Percival advocated a whole-person approach to the patient ("the feelings and emotions of the patients . . . require to be known and attended to, no less than the symptoms of the disease"), recommended that the poor receive free or discounted care, insisted that medicine be a research science constantly seeking new and better approaches, and even dictated the still-prevailing academic custom that a junior physician deliver his opinion first at the bedside. As to business, Percival simply cautions physicians to "guard against whatever may injure the general respectability of the profession." At another point he says, "the characteristic beneficence of the profession is inconsistent with sordid views and avaricious rapacity." The AMA code endorses these views and adds that advertising and the solicitation of patients are "derogatory to the dignity of the profession," both activities being "highly reprehensible in a regular physician."

Dr. Thomas Percival's *Code of Medical Ethics* (1803) became the basis for much of the AMA's *Principles of Medical Ethics.*

This injunction, in one form or another, remained in the AMA's professional code through numerous revisions across the years. It is not hard to see how the ethical ban on solicitation—imprinted along with the rest of the profession's accepted wisdoms on some four generations of American physicians—became more than just an idea on paper. By the time a young and energetic Sidney Garfield appeared on the medical scene, the AMA's *Principles* had the presence—if not the force—of law.

The Federal Trade Commission (FTC) is a unique government agency with far-reaching authority to independently investigate, prosecute, and render censures for violations of antitrust law. Established in 1914, the agency was charged at the outset with enforcing the Sherman and Clayton acts, the foundations of antitrust law. The guiding philosophy behind these acts is that competitive markets must be protected and preserved; such self-regulation in business works to the advantage of both buyer and seller. The language of the Sherman Act provides a general sense of purpose, declaring illegal "every contract, combination in the form of trust or otherwise, or conspiracy, in restraint of trade."

Along with a panel of five commissioners, the FTC relies on three administrative law judges and can bring its own administrative cases for in-house hearing and decision. Although any FTC decision may be appealed in federal court, it can be an uphill battle for the defendants; their alleged transgressions have already been investigated and decided upon.

The commission has had a rather variable history, usually colored by the politics of its chairman and, beyond that, the general directives of the president who appoints him. When President Carter named Michael Pertschuk chairman in 1976, he knew that Pertschuk wanted the commission to wade into the deep waters of the old, vested interests in American economic life, seeking to discover the conflicts of interest and cozy deals left in place by previous presidents. Not surprisingly, this was easier said than done.

One of these interests was the organized practice of medicine, as represented by the American Medical Association and its many affiliate societies around the nation. As precedents for its investigation, the FTC could cite not only *D.C. Medical Society* v. *Group Health Association*, but also *Goldfarb* v. *Virginia State Bar.*

Lewis Goldfarb was in the process of buying a family home in the suburbs of Washington, D.C., in 1971, when he found that the minimum attorney's fee for conducting a title search was the same all over the area, no matter where he inquired. Goldfarb learned that the fee consistently quoted by numerous lawyers was precisely what the area bar association dictated. He had discovered what was, in effect, a price-fixing scheme among professionals. Price-fixing specifically violates antitrust laws, and Goldfarb sued the bar association. When the Supreme Court ruled on the suit in 1975, it declared that the legal profession was subject to the Sherman Act.

Before *Goldfarb*, the learned professions had enjoyed a long-standing, tacit exemption from FTC jurisdiction, a sort of untested gentlemen's agreement. Now it was clear that all the professions could fall under similar antitrust rulings.

The stage for bringing a case against the AMA was neatly

Doctors getting a dose of their own medicine was a common theme in editorial cartoons about *AMA* v. *FTC*. Several U.S. newspapers ran this one, by Jeff MacNelly, in 1978.

set. On December 19, 1975, FTC staff attorneys brought a complaint before administrative law judge Ernest G. Barnes, claiming the AMA had consistently violated antitrust laws by conspiring with its local affiliates to prevent competition between doctors and to hinder solicitation of business and advertising. The complaint said the AMA's ideological authority for the alleged preventions and hindrances was the time-honored *Principles of Medical Ethics.*

Ernest Barnes is now retired from the Federal Trade Commission. He remembers "the AMA affair" as a major undertaking, one of the most significant decisions of his career. "Doctors thought they were above the law," he told me when I visited him at his home in Maryland not long ago.

The judge showed me a scrapbook of clippings he had kept on the case, drawing my attention first to a political cartoon by Jeff MacNelly. In it, a doctor labeled FTC holds aloft a huge hypodermic needle labeled ADVERTISING. Waiting to one side with trousers dropped is an anxious figure labeled AMA.

Judge Barnes pointed to the cartoon, smiling. "Here's a terrific summary of the case," he said. "The shoe was on the other foot, and the doctors didn't like it. Not one little bit."

I asked about the ethical perspective, the principled idea that a profession like medicine would be demeaned and trivialized by the incursion of price competition and advertising. The judge shook his head.

"Didn't hold up," he said. "Still doesn't. For one thing, the Supreme Court had already advised us that a profession can't hide behind ethics when it told the National Society of Professional Engineers to stop its prohibition on competitive bidding as an unethical practice. Then there's the simple reality of life in the business world. The AMA wanted to pretend doctors were on the highest pedestal, that the business they were in bore no connection to everybody else's business."

Judge Barnes waved a hand, bemused.

"Because they all went to medical school, they're finer human beings than the rest of us? No longer subject to the laws of the United States?"

Judge Barnes's scrapbook is filled with reports on the case, profiles of himself, other political cartoons lampooning the case's details, and his final order in 1979. "Of course, it didn't end there. The AMA appealed it."

Had the judge ever had any concern about a reversal of his decision on appeal? I asked. He laughed.

"No way," he said. "It's a matter of legal precedent. The Supreme Court had already decided in favor of the antitrust side in four other cases. Why would they suddenly change their minds?"

When asked for a general overview of the case, Judge Barnes closed his scrapbook and studied its cover for a moment. "The AMA would have you think we didn't care about medical ethics or the inherent risks in out-of-control marketing or misleading advertising," he said. "But that's not true. The FTC never intended for organized medicine to abandon everything they stood for, only that ethical considerations be reasonable. There's the important word. Reasonable."

"You know," he continued, "prohibiting commercial activity doesn't save a profession from its own worst enemies. Allowing doctors to openly compete and generally commer-

Retired judge Ernest G. Barnes, photographed during a 1991 visit to the National Arboretum in Washington, D.C., says *AMA* v. *FTC* was the most important decision of his career.

cialize their practices doesn't mean there will suddenly be more quacks or incompetents or outright liars. They've always been there. Ethics don't mean a thing to those types, anyway. On the other hand, the commercial prohibition did suppress a flow of appropriate information about health-care services and, more importantly, it blocked innovation and change.

"It's a benefits-outweighing-the-risks kind of situation," Judge Barnes said. "I think the FTC made it possible for organized medicine to get out of the 19th century, to get on with things." Scrapbook back in place, the judge turned and said,

"I think opening the door to commercialization was one of the best things to happen to our health-care system."

The principal attorneys representing the AMA (and, by extension, all of American medicine) throughout the FTC hearing and appeals were Newton Minow and Jack Bierig. Minow, a longtime associate of Democratic Party leader Adlai Stevenson, served as chairman of the Federal Communications Commission in John F. Kennedy's administration and is remembered for his remark "Television is a vast wasteland." Recalling the case as a "disaster" for organized medicine, Minow said, "the FTC was busy trying to force the economist's view of life on a group of people that didn't want it. If Hippocrates were alive today, the FTC would sue him."

Jack Bierig, the primary trial counsel in the FTC-AMA proceeding, refers to the case as "the biggest thing on my plate between December of 1975 and March of 1982." Just as *Goldfarb* had helped precipitate the case against the AMA, *Bates* v. *State Bar of Arizona*, a case decided two years later, served to further encourage the FTC. In *Bates*, the court held that advertising ("commercial speech") by lawyers could not be banned by state bar associations.

"*Bates* was a major development which spurred the FTC on," Bierig said. A complicating factor, however, was that the AMA had revised—and eased—its prohibition against physician advertising two months before the *Bates* case reached the Supreme Court. "The AMA knew about *Goldfarb*, and they knew there were antitrust implications to their conduct. And they saw the *Bates* case coming and were thoughtful and tried to respond to the times."

But the FTC refused to judge the AMA on the basis of its revised standards. "They wanted to get a victim," Bierig said.

Jimmy Carter entered office in 1977 with a sense that old wrongs might be righted, that the house of government would be cleaned once and for all. The AMA was perceived as an exclusive society closing ranks to protect the dark corners of its trade—and its very sizable income. No one was surprised when the FTC accused the AMA of conspiracy.

Although all the FTC attorneys to whom I spoke took great

pains to establish that the word *conspiracy* is not pejorative, the fact remains that it denotes a partnership toward an illicit goal. Legally speaking, one of the lawyers told me, it can be an action that turns out to be illegal, even if that was not the original intention. The FTC saw the AMA's *Principles*, a document that directed its local affiliate societies to enact the rules of the parent organization, as an instrument of conspiracy.

Much more damning, however, were documents subpoenaed from the AMA that seemed to constitute active enforcement "recommendations" made by the AMA to the numerous local societies. These communications generally took the form of opinions from the AMA Judicial Council advising the local societies to conform with and enforce the *Principles of Medical Ethics.*

"Once we got a chance to see the AMA's files," said Dan Barney, one of the FTC staff attorneys involved with the AMA case, "we found a plethora of correspondence and internal memoranda and other smoking-gun documents showing actual and extensive enforcement of these prohibitory principles."

Jack Bierig disagrees: "There was no evidence that any physician was ever sanctioned by the AMA as a result of violating the principles of ethics."

As in so many legal wrangles, the point is a finely drawn technicality. Both men are correct, and this cleavage in interpretation characterized a case freighted with "evidence" that could be seen in opposite lights, depending on one's personal philosophy.

Witness the 1974 incident involving Washington State ophthalmologist Cyril Lundvick, cited by the FTC in its complaint. Lundvick wanted to announce a new practice location in the greater Seattle area. A one-inch announcement giving his name, address, and specialty appeared in a local newspaper.

Responding to a member's complaint, the Kitsap County Medical Society determined Lundvick's "ad" to be unethical. Lundvick was so advised. The authority cited was the AMA's *Opinions and Reports* (1971). The ophthalmologist's attention was directed to this passage: "The practice of medicine should not be commercialized nor treated as a commodity in trade. Respecting the dignity of their calling, physicians should resort only to the most limited use of advertising."

What, one might readily ask, is more "limited" than a one-inch announcement in a daily paper? In any event, payments of Lundvick's insurance claims were withheld until he canceled his announcement and agreed never to do such a thing again.

Here, then, was a rather amazing example of how rigid and patently unreasonable a local medical society could become in applying the edicts of the AMA. There is little doubt that Lundvick was sanctioned. Withholding an individual's income as a punitive measure cannot be seen as anything else.

He was not, however, sanctioned directly by the AMA, but by an affiliate society, which enforced the AMA's *Principles* in a manner so crudely belligerent as to be dismissive of the basic rights of a citizen. The question of how the AMA's Judicial Council would have handled the case had Lundvick come before the council directly is moot.

Art Lerner, another attorney assigned to the AMA case during his tenure at the FTC, explains that for him the crux of the FTC's position was the AMA's fundamental conspiracy to censure. Imagine a doctor joining the AMA through a local affiliate, says Lerner. The doctor is accepted into membership on the condition there be no solicitation of patients and no advertising. The doctor knowingly enters into that agreement, Lerner observes, thereby becoming both participant in and, possibly, victim of a pledge to enforce the rules of the profession. Since this particular agreement violates Section 5 of the Federal Trade Commission Act, it is unlawful conspiracy.

Following this reasoning, the lack of specific evidence for face-to-face censure of physicians by the AMA Judicial Council was irrelevant. The intention and the means were there, in the form of the ethical code. Conspiracy, Lerner admits, "is a nefarious term, and the AMA took great offense at it . . . but it really was not a tough question, as a matter of law."

If the AMA's dignity was injured, the fact remained that, just as the FTC insisted, individual doctors like Cyril Lundvick—as well as creative medical-care alternatives like prepaid health plans—were being sanctioned and repressed by the aggressive application of the AMA's *Principles.* One of the more extreme examples of AMA-influenced censure occurred around the same time as the Lundvick affair. It is the rather sad tale of

Medi-Call, a house-call service in Johnson County, Kansas.

The premise of the service was simple and innovative. For an annual fee, subscribers would have access to a rotating staff of physicians who would make house calls in the suburban area. The physicians would be part-time employees of Medi-Call (no physicians were owners, and none acted as managers), and the service would meet at least some of the health-care needs of the area. Medi-Call's owners took special care to work with the local medical society by asking for advice on appropriate advertising before the start-up of business.

The owners were told that advertising was acceptable, provided none of the physicians were mentioned by name. Medi-Call agreed. Radio, television, newspaper, and billboard advertising began; subscribers were enrolled. Local opinion was quite favorable toward this new service that could fill the needs of the elderly and the housebound. Then Medi-Call executives received a letter from the Kansas City-based Area Medical Council advising them they were engaged in activities that were both unethical and illegal.

Unethical? Medi-Call was a privately owned business, with no physician investors or partners. Illegal? This term was left undefined in the council's letter. Medi-Call took the matter to Vern Miller, the attorney general of the State of Kansas.

Miller responded that the Area Medical Council's notions were nonsense. He issued an opinion that formally declared there to be nothing even faintly illegal in Medi-Call's operation. But that wasn't good enough for Dr. C. Y. Thomas, spokesman for the Area Medical Council. "The legal opinions of Vern Miller have nothing to do with our canons of ethics," he told Medi-Call.

Thomas was reminded by Medi-Call's lawyers that Miller was, after all, the attorney general. "Now listen here," the doctor roared back. "You might be legal but we're still declaring you unethical . . . the fact that you're legal doesn't influence me at all. Now if you want to criticize the system that brought me up to believe this, then criticize it. But your client doesn't know the canons of ethics, and that's that. He needs the book read to him, and that's what we're doing. You understand that?"

Not long after the meeting in which Thomas made his feel-

Kansas Attorney General Vern Miller's office took on the area AMA affiliate when it tried to shut down Medi-Call, a house-call service, in 1973.

*"I have worked as hard as I could...
if my success has been greater than
that of most...the reason is that I came
in my wanderings through the medical field upon regions where the gold
was still lying by the wayside...and
that is of no great merit."*

Miles is proud to present this series on...

Powerful Innovators

Powerful Physician

Robert Koch (1843-1910)

Even Koch himself would have been surprised to learn in 1866 that he would become one of the most important bacteriologists of all time. His dream of traveling to exotic ports took an ironic turn when his wife's gift of a microscope spurred his interest in the exotic world of microbes.

With a passionate interest in bacteriology generated by a crisis that struck in 1876 (an anthrax epidemic among local cattle), Koch studied the disease, cultured the organism on artificial media, analyzed its complete life cycle, and transferred the infection to mice.

Koch's research in bacteriology continued: He isolated and cultivated staphylococci from surgical infections, analyzed streptococci taken from wound exudate, and discovered the bacillus that causes conjunctivitis. Perhaps his most important contribution was the discovery of the bacillus responsible for tuberculosis, a devastating illness at that time.

Powerful Antimicrobial

Today, in lower respiratory infections,* some pathogens are no longer routinely susceptible to traditional agents. That's why today's pulmonologist needs Cipro®, with the power to eradicate a broad spectrum of pathogens, from Streptococcus pneumoniae *to* Klebsiella pneumoniae, *from* Pseudomonas aeruginosa *to* Haemophilus influenzae. *Even many difficult gram-negative pathogens are no match for the power of Cipro® .*

Cipro® TABLETS
(ciprofloxacin HCl)

The most potent fluoroquinolone.[1-3†]

* Due to susceptible strains of indicated pathogens. See indicated organisms in prescribing information.
†In vitro activity does not necessarily imply a correlation with in vivo results.

See full prescribing information at the end of this book.

Powerful Numbers

Speak for themselves

5 *...The number of indications for which Cipro® is indicated: lower respiratory infections, skin and skin structure infections, bone and joint infections, urinary tract infections, infectious diarrhea.**

12 *...Number of hours serum concentrations of Cipro® are maintained in excess of $MIC_{90}s$ of most susceptible bacteria.*

96 *...The percentage of favorable clinical response (resolution + improvement) with Cipro® in lower respiratory infections due to susceptible strains of indicated pathogens.*

250/500/750 *...Dosage strengths of Cipro® Tablets available.*

Cipro® TABLETS

(ciprofloxacin HCl)

The most potent fluoroquinolone.[1-3†]

CIPRO® SHOULD NOT BE USED IN CHILDREN, ADOLESCENTS, OR PREGNANT WOMEN.

See full prescribing information at the end of this book.

COMMITTED TO THERAPEUTIC EFFICIENCY

MILES

Miles Inc.
Pharmaceutical Division
400 Morgan Lane
West Haven, CT 06516

© March 1991, Miles Inc. Pharmaceutical Division   Printed in U.S.A.   CD9570H ings clear, the Area Medical Council wrote to the AMA for its opinion of the matter—and enclosed Attorney General Miller's opinion. The AMA's official response upheld the council's position: legality, said the letter, had no necessary bearing on medical judgment.

In upholding C. Y. Thomas's smug conceit, the AMA offered a vivid example of the arrogance that has burdened the profession in so many crises. In this case, the AMA allowed the pious personal opinions of a few doctors to undermine a valuable opportunity to improve patient care. Nor would the Area Medical Council let the matter rest. Its persistent disruption and harassment generated the negative environment its members hoped for: Medi-Call's executives gave up. So it was that the AMA's prohibition on advertising was used to help destroy a private, legally operated business that represented an innovation in health care.

As with the Lundvick case, the AMA had not directly caused Medi-Call's failure. Still, the demise of Medi-Call shows a professional association exercising inappropriate power and operating well beyond its purview. It was only a matter of time before such tyrannies would be challenged in court in a case of far-reaching implications for both medicine and society at large.

If Judge Ernest Barnes could later make the remark that "doctors thought they were above the law," he had certainly been given reasonable grounds for his perception.

CHAPTER FOUR

AMA vs. FTC

ollowing the filing of the complaint with Judge Barnes in late 1975, lawyers for the FTC began the work of legal discovery. Their first hurdle was to demonstrate that the FTC indeed held jurisdiction over the AMA—a nonprofit professional association. This was the make-or-break issue. Despite the Supreme Court's decisions in the *Goldfarb* and *Bates* cases, the learned professions had yet to be taken to task by the government in any large-scale legal action. At stake was the FTC's dominion over the professions in general. A victory would reorient the government's legal stance toward all the professions. Engineers and accountants, lawyers and architects—and doctors—would henceforth have to accept that their occupations were subject to antitrust law.

The burden of proof rested with the Federal Trade Commission. If the agency had jurisdiction over the professions, that authority had to be adequately demonstrated. If not, the FTC's case would be worthless. The FTC team worked for months researching the economic world of American medicine. Team members pored over cartons of subpoenaed documents, reviewed financial records, and compiled a history of the AMA. Friendly and unfriendly witnesses were deposed.

The issue of jurisdiction was one of the major issues throughout the proceedings. Testimony was presented by two economists, Frederick Sturdivant and Paul Feldstein. Sturdivant, the AMA's witness, maintained that the AMA met the test for nonprofit status because it did not exist to advance the monetary interests of its membership. Feldstein, speaking for the FTC, advised Judge Barnes that such was not the case: a careful analysis of financial records and spending patterns showed the AMA to be preoccupied with expanding the wealth of its members.

The second and perhaps most important area of concern was the argument over medical advertising's potential for deception. This was the single most potent issue of the general controversy over medical commercialization, and nowhere else in the case were the arguments for and against quite so emotional and symbolic.

The AMA's Jack Bierig hoped that the debate about medical marketing's capacity for deception and fraud would break the case open. "It was perhaps our most significant line of defense," Bierig told me when I visited him in Chicago. "We argued that advertising by physicians had a tremendous potential for deception."

The AMA, he said, wanted an out-of-court settlement in which it would agree to accept the FTC's authority in every area save one: It wanted to continue to police false and misleading advertising by physicians.

"The analogy in constant use was that of the fox guarding the chicken coop," Bierig said. "Physicians were, in the FTC's eyes, not interested in the public welfare, and so physicians and medical societies should have no role whatsoever in regulating advertising." To completely deprive medical societies of any regulatory or enforcement authority would render them little more than social clubs, Bierig asserted. Such a humbling transformation "was totally contrary to what the societies felt was their proper role. And, in my view, it was a completely arbitrary position for the FTC."

FTC attorney Art Lerner contends that Bierig and the AMA never had a leg to stand on. To take the position that advertising posed an unacceptable risk to medicine and its consumers was, in light of precedents, "legally indefensible." In other words, restricting advertising equaled restricting trade, which was, pure and simple, against the law. Lerner also saw the AMA's concern about the more conceptual and philosophical aspects of medical practice—aspects like the doctor-patient relationship—as interesting material for intellectual discussion, but lacking the clean edges necessary for legal

Barry Costilo (left), chief counsel for the FTC, chats with Newton Minow, lead attorney for the AMA, before the start of the 1977 hearings on physician-advertising restrictions.

argument. Lerner felt that these concerns were "fundamentally inadmissible" in court.

In any event, to have settled these matters out of court would have deprived the FTC of a high-profile accomplishment: extending and fully establishing the government's jurisdiction over all of the learned professions. This was an all-or-nothing affair.

The AMA's stratagem for convincing Judge Barnes of the danger in lifting the organization's prohibition on solicitation was to show him victims—people who had suffered because they believed a deceptive medical advertisment. Their stories were uniformly tragic, and Bierig intended to use them to lift his argument out of the abstract and into the realm of tangible human concerns.

This he did handily: the AMA's witnesses recounted horrendous medical travesties. All were victims of cosmetic surgery come-ons, and had undergone assaults that were beyond the pale: unethical prescription of narcotics and tranquilizers; multiple clumsy surgeries attempting to correct an initial clumsy surgery; resulting physical impairments that should have cost the responsible surgeons lifetime suspensions from the practice of medicine.

Bierig's witnesses described a world of physicians who used simplistic advertisements to promise stellar body (and life) improvements through plastic surgery.

One woman—the AMA's Consumer Witness Number One—had responded to an ad published in the *Los Angeles Times* in 1976 that told her "cosmetic surgery can give you what nature didn't." She went to see "Maurice and Vicky" at the "Women's Advisory Council," who admitted they were a front operation "representing doctors." The witness was then given a frank sales pitch on the merits and benefits of breast implants and was referred to a Dr. Lipton. She claimed she was told there were "no risks" involved.

Having decided to go through with the surgery, she found herself in a hospital that she described as "a dirty, horrible place." When she awoke after surgery, the nurse was abusive and the surroundings were squalid. In short order, it became apparent that her surgery had been botched. The witness testified that she had to endure eight more surgeries over nearly two more years (with two other doctors), that she suffered harrowing drug reactions as well as a case of gangrene, and that she spent $20,000 in medical fees—all because of a seductive newspaper advertisement.

"It was very moving testimony," recalls Barry Costilo, the FTC's chief trial counsel on the case. "You could hear a pin drop in that courtroom." Did it prove that all medical advertising should be prohibited? Costilo leaned back in his chair and considered the question.

"Well, these unfortunate women that Jack Bierig presented were tragic situations. Nobody would ever deny that. But it was also a legal gambit designed to get everybody's emotions involved. The real question remained: Was economic competition a bad thing in health care? Police incompetent doctors, by all means. But prohibit legitimate business practices by reputable doctors? That's another, much larger question."

Those questions would be addressed with a second legal approach: the presentation of testimony by important American physicians who had opinions about medical advertising.

Dr. Michael Halberstam testified as an expert witness for the AMA. He said advertising by physicians should not be allowed.

The late Dr. Michael Halberstam was one of medicine's most distinguished voices. A celebrated internist, clinical professor, medical journalist, and member of the National Academy of Sciences' Institute of Medicine, Halberstam told the court that advertising by physicians would unquestionably harm patients and society in general.

Jack Bierig asked precisely how advertising might be harmful. Halberstam replied that physicians would feel pressure to view their practices as commodities, to look for the easy-to-solve problems and the high yield.

"I think," Halberstam testified, "that advertising can't help but erode and eventually destroy the concept of professionalism." Mentioning that some of his best friends were businessmen, Halberstam went on to point out the difference between businessmen and professionals. "The object of a business is to maximize profits, whereas one of the touchstones of professionalism is that one is not trying to maximize one's profit or one's income."

Halberstam acknowledged that there are business components to medical practice but observed that the pivotal distinction in a professional's business behavior is the rationale for refusing a client. In the case of a doctor, there is the routine possibility that a patient must be turned away for ethical reasons alone. Perhaps the patient's illness is so minimal that treatment is unwarranted. Perhaps the illness is beyond the doctor's experience, or should be treated by a different specialist. Whatever the reason, a professional will send the patient away. A businessman, Halberstam speculated, focuses on the client's income potential, and would be less likely to decline any case.

Halberstam also claimed medical advertising had created a "burden of neurosis" for the American people, and referred to an essay by the eminent physician Lewis Thomas. Thomas maintained that completely legitimate ads from organizations like the American Cancer Society and the American Heart Association had created a market for disease. Halberstam thought that increasing the competitive mentality among medical organizations and physicians would accelerate this marketplace for illness, creating "a feeling that we are born ill and have to be made well."

The FTC's expert, Dr. Robert Ebert, argued that banning advertising by physicians stifled the public's access to information about health care.

When Barry Costilo telephoned Dr. Robert Ebert, he did so with a bit of trepidation. It was a cold call, based on earlier word that Ebert just might be the man to testify for the FTC. Robert Higgins Ebert was as eminent and widely known a physician as was Michael Halberstam. Now retired, he was president of the Milbank Memorial Fund at the time of the hearing and had been dean of Harvard Medical School for 12 years, a Rhodes scholar, and chairman of the Board of Regents of the National Library of Medicine. But Costilo was worried: why should a distinguished physician care to argue against the tenets of his own profession?

Ebert was, in fact, hesitant to testify when he first heard Costilo's explanation of the case and its broad implications, but he finally assented. As it turned out, he did have a few things to say, not only about physician advertising, but about the entire spectrum of medicine's commercialization.

As soon as Ebert took the witness stand and was asked if he held any opinions regarding physician advertising, Bierig objected. Dr. Ebert's medical credentials were indeed impressive, he said, but no foundation had been laid for his expertise in the area of medical advertising.

Judge Barnes overruled the objection. Bierig countered, asserting that, after all, Michael Halberstam had consistently demonstrated his expertise on questions of medical advertising through his writing. Barnes again overruled the objection, finding the witness to be "certainly more qualified than I am," and allowing Ebert to move forward with the opinion that advertising should be permitted among physicians.

For Ebert, the first problem in prohibiting solicitation and advertising was that it stifled information about medicine and health care. "I think patients are often unaware of the choices that are available to them, and in part that is because their physicians have not advertised," Ebert testified. He elaborated on the large system that medical care had become, a labyrinthine network of interlocking specialties. Without information, he said, consumers are denied access to and knowledge of a system that, ostensibly at least, exists to serve their needs.

As Costilo's examination proceeded, Bierig objected several times, continuing to challenge Ebert's credentials as an expert on questions regarding medical advertising and commercialism. In each case, he was overruled. Ebert continued to expand on his initial points, suggesting that advertising could be seen as a form of public education, a way of empowering consumers without injuring the medical profession; thus the examination arrived at the much-debated definition of a "professional."

Robert Ebert offered a revisionist view of professionalism among doctors. The fundamental premise in clinical practice, he told the court, was and has always been the physician's concern for the patient's welfare. This is the single "general professional ethic of the physician—a rather deeply ingrained one." As long as the patient's welfare was not sacrificed or compromised, professionalism prevailed and would suffer little damage from the inroads of commercialism.

But even with patients' interests firmly safeguarded, what of the risk of deception in advertising by physicians? Ebert said he believed this tendency would be offset by two strong and simple deterrents: the basic ethical feelings most physicians harbor about their work, and their fear of malpractice suits.

"[Should] the AMA and medical societies police doctors through the device of advertising restrictions?" Costilo asked Ebert.

Bierig objected again, pointing out that that question was ultimately what the entire case would decide, and "not on the basis of Dr. Ebert's speculation."

Barnes again overruled the objection, accepting Bierig's

observation but reminding him that speculation need not be accepted as fact in the final analysis. Costilo urged Ebert to continue.

As Costilo and Bierig fought for the moral high ground, the testimonies of Dr. Robert Ebert and Dr. Michael Halberstam became the focus of the case. It seemed that everything in the embattled relationship between commerce and medicine turned on the arguments of these two men. The case had arrived at the problem of what the truth might be. And by whose lights the truth should be assessed.

Costilo conducted Ebert across the landscape of the case, creating a kind of thumbnail history of medical commercialism. There was the AMA's notion that unregulated advertising would allow an avalanche of false (and silly) claims by quacks. Ebert observed that such advertising has never been within the purview of medical societies, and besides, the public's ability to assess advertising was underestimated. To posit an overwhelming need for public protection from misleading ads, said Ebert, was symptomatic of medicine's arrogance. There is the problem of advertising the price of procedures, Costilo pointed out. Some say it will influence people to buy cheaper medical care rather than to choose higher quality. Ebert thought not: For one thing, he noted, there's health insurance. For another, citizens have an undeniable right to know what things will cost.

Costilo raised another argument: commercializing medicine might irreparably damage the doctor-patient relationship. Ebert observed that the various attacks the profession had endured over the years had not actually done much to hurt the doctor-patient relationship. He cited a 1978 Robert Wood Johnson Foundation study that found undiminished confidence in one's personal physician even if the respondent felt critical of the profession in general.

Finally, Costilo returned to deception in medical ads, with the clear intent to link all the points discussed to that pivotal concern. Bierig objected again. To allow an answer, he argued, would be to allow further speculation and would be "going beyond anything that is proper under the rules of evidence."

Costilo considered the situation a moment—and decided

to let the matter rest. He advised the judge he had no further questions.

On cross-examination, Bierig focused closely on the question of deception, with an intensive line of questions about the ads that had led Bierig's earlier witnesses—the victims of incompetent cosmetic surgeons—into such difficulties. The ads beckoned with headlines like IMPROVE YOUR APPEARANCE; YOU DON'T HAVE TO BE RICH TO MAKE THE MOST OF YOURSELF; and I'M A NEW WOMAN! Bierig asked Ebert if he thought consumers knew enough to judge such ads.

Yes, Ebert thought, given the tawdry nature of the advertising, the exaggerated claims, the generally suspicious "feel" of the ads.

Bierig was not convinced. Couldn't such advertising mislead? Couldn't it draw the unsuspecting into medical situations that were inappropriate or, in the worst case, tragic? Certainly, Ebert conceded, but that presupposed other complexities: people who wanted to be misled, who were locked into emotional or psychological downturns that made wild medical offers seem attractive. "The character of these ads is such that the majority of consumers would not be misled," Ebert testified.

Bierig continued to hammer at the problem of deceptive advertising's potential for luring the innocent and the uninformed. Ebert finally said he didn't believe advertising, in and of itself, was all that important. What finally matters, he said, is what a physician actually does in promoting a practice and caring for patients, and those actions, not advertising, are what might call for formal evaluation and regulation. Ebert never denied medical advertising's potential for abuse—the evidence was abundant—but he insisted that Bierig's clippings were only isolated examples of blatant irresponsibility. It would be wrong, he thought, to suppress every type of solicitation and marketing on the basis of such evidence. "What is difficult," Ebert told the court, "are the gray areas. There is the unfortunate tendency to regulate more severely those things you don't happen to personally like, so the principle of prohibiting advertising is a dangerous one."

On October 12, 1979, Judge Ernest G. Barnes ordered the AMA "to cease engaging in any action that would restrict its members' solicitation of patients by advertising."

The AMA appealed the decision to the Second Circuit Court of Appeals. One member of the three-judge panel, Walter R. Mansfield, dissented from the majority opinion, noting that because the AMA had indeed updated its ethical guidelines before the FTC initiated its complaint, the entire case was invalid. The FTC, he said, was "pressing for its pound of flesh," engaging in "the futile business of beating a dead horse." Mansfield also commented on the "mootness" of the issues involved, calling the FTC's complaint "unjustified, unnecessary, and a waste of administrative and judicial resources." Finally, Judge Mansfield characterized the FTC's conduct as "an abuse of discretion." The remaining two judges on the Second Circuit concurred with Judge Barnes's ruling. The case then went to the U.S. Supreme Court, where, in March 1982, Barnes's original order was affirmed by a 4-4 vote, with Justice Harry Blackmun abstaining.

It was all over. The FTC had maintained the advantage throughout. The courts had formally determined that the AMA had conspired to suppress competition among doctors, and that there was a danger that such illegal activity might recur. The Barnes decision would reshape American medicine.

In spite of the Supreme Court's affirmation of the Barnes ruling, many points of the case remain arguable today. The AMA, after all, had updated and liberalized its ethical guidelines before the initiation of the FTC complaint. The dangerous capacity of unregulated physician advertising to mislead seems abundantly clear. This problem came under large-scale congressional scrutiny later in the 1980s and continues to concern thoughtful physicians everywhere. Then there is the original question of FTC jurisdiction: Jack Bierig pointed to a recent case in which it was held that the FTC did not have jurisdiction over a nonprofit hospital. "So this issue is still quite alive," he said.

Bierig recalled Judge Barnes as "exceedingly slanted" toward a positive outcome for the FTC. "I looked at the person who tried the case with me," Bierig told me, "and I had to ask if Ernest Barnes was sitting in the same courtroom we were, because there was clear evidence that the old, restrictive AMA rules were motivated by an assumption that physician advertising had a great potential for deception that outweighed any benefits. And in practice there was no evidence that allowing advertising by physicians would in fact lower prices or increase output or do any of the things the antitrust laws are designed to do."

Bierig paused, looking toward the wraparound windows of his 49th-floor office. For a moment silence lingered above the muted noise of traffic from the streets below. When Bierig continued it was to say that Judge Barnes's decision bore virtually no relationship to the facts presented in the case: "Judge Barnes, I think, had blinders on. He was determined to find for the FTC."

The FTC's refusal to compromise in any way was "inexcusable," in Bierig's view, representing "a zealotry that should be unacceptable. And I must say, if one looks at the world today, one has to ask, Is the patient better off as a result of physician advertising?"

I talked with Dr. Robert Ebert in the early summer of 1991, 13 years after he had taken the witness stand on behalf of the FTC. Looking back, Ebert told me, he finds that "the uses of advertising in medicine have gone in the general direction I suggested in my testimony. Indeed, if we are to retain a mixed system of medical care, it's inevitable that there will be continued attempts to persuade the public to use one form of care over another."

Ebert recalled the trial with quiet good humor. He acknowledged that *hammer* would be the appropriate word to describe Bierig's approach to cross-examination. "The AMA's argument was so narrow, it seems to me they were bound to lose," Ebert said. "It was as if the only thing implied by the term *commercial* was fraudulent advertising."

The AMA used advertising as a "whipping boy," Ebert thought, to such an extent that it became "an artificial issue." It is ironic, Ebert reminded me, that he has since been a vocal critic of medical commercialism, of its unfettered growth and questionable extremes. But, he adds, "unless we have some sort of national health service, it's inescapable."

"The AMA is a lot more skillful today," Ebert said. "It's a

changed organization. They have a more enlightened leadership." The old concerns for solicitation have been fully laid to rest, in Ebert's view.

After all, he observed, this very book is a project made possible by advertising. "The commercialization of medicine," he said, "is now an established part of our culture."

CHAPTER FIVE

AFTER THE FALL

on Wyden is, at 42, an 11-year veteran of Congress, the Democratic representative from Oregon's Third District. As chairman of the House Subcommittee on Regulation, Business Opportunities, and Energy, he has directed a series of aggressive investigations into "post-FTC" medical marketing.

They began in 1989, when Wyden asked the subcommittee staff to draft a report. "Although we have found that most in the medical community are honest and ethical," the report said, "many are not. Whether it be consumers counting on safe, reliable medical testing, infertile couples seeking to have a baby, or those seeing lumps or bumps in the mirror, all are highly susceptible to potential exploitation." Since then, subcommittee probes have examined in vitro fertilization, abuses in cosmetic surgery, interstate medical franchises, fraudulent advertising, and regulatory concerns at both state and federal levels. Wyden has been vocal in his criticism of the Federal Trade Commission's role in helping to create these problems, and he contends that the agency's support for unrestrained advertising by the medical profession gave "the green light to charlatans and hucksters."

Steve Jenning is the staff director of Wyden's subcommittee. I found him walled in by filing cabinets in a windowless basement room of the Rayburn House Office Building. When I introduced myself, describing the reason for my visit and the purpose of this book, Jenning immediately began a harried search for the appropriate hearing transcripts. He spoke as he rummaged through drawers, banging them open and closed.

"The FTC," he said. "What are they up to? They actually had

a guy admit some people could be lost with the push to bring advertising into medicine. Can you believe that?"

Jenning was having some trouble locating the transcripts. He stood on his chair to reach into a cabinet above his desk. "Think about it," he said. "Here's a government agency that thinks human life can be exchanged for a certain view of the law."

The chair Jenning was standing on began to slide; he stepped up onto his desk and pushed his head into the cabinet. He called out to an associate on the other side of the filing-cabinet wall. He wanted to know where a particular box of transcripts might be. The associate shrugged. Jenning turned to me and said, "The in vitro transcripts were a hit. We haven't been able to keep them around."

I said that I recalled that Congressman Wyden had claimed the FTC had "simply diddled" when faced with overt problems in medical marketing. Jenning nodded vigorously, stepping from one desktop to another, straddling the open space between them. "Absolutely. The FTC started something here they haven't followed through on." He found a transcript and tossed it down to me.

"See, the FTC told doctors it was okay to advertise, to market themselves, to invest in partnerships, all that. But when you do that, you know there'll be abuses, profiteers. So you have to be ready to deal with the problems you create. And that's where the FTC has failed." He rummaged through another box, talking all the while. "We know the majority of doctors aren't intentionally defrauding or injuring anybody. But that leaves a minority who have taken advantage of this loose environment the FTC has given us. And consumers have a right to be protected from that minority."

Jenning jumped down from his desktop, and I asked if he thought that American medicine was in deeper trouble than ever before as a result of the FTC victory in 1982.

"I think so," he said. "Medicine deals with human beings, after all. Not some manufacturer's product line."

What's the solution?

"There's the rub, right?" Jenning collapsed into the chair he had been standing on. "Legislation, agreements, cease-and-desist orders, things like that. I mean, we're not talking about creating another federal layer here. It's a lot of small actions that increase regulatory postures, that protect the consumer, that keep people from getting hurt."

Although the routine purview of the House Subcommittee on Regulation, Business Opportunities, and Energy includes medical marketing, another event underscores Ron Wyden's focus on extremes in clinical advertising: the death of Mary Church.

Representative Ron Wyden (D-Ore.) has held a series of hearings on abuses of medical advertising in the post-FTC era.

Mary Church, 64, was a constituent of Wyden's from Portland who in 1988 responded to a newspaper advertisement offering a chemical face peel. This is a legitimate procedure in the hands of appropriately trained plastic surgeons and dermatologists. In this case, however, the doctor was a suburban general practitioner who had attended a one-week "see one, do one" workshop on the peel. Following the application of the peel solution (a phenol compound), Mary Church was "discharged" to a motel room. It was there that she died in diabetic ketoacidosis, with no doctor in attendance.

The marketer who sold the "see one, do one" face-peel package, Michael Walerstein, solicited physicians' business through direct mail, using a "Dear Doctor" form letter that promised physicians who added the procedure to their services a gain of as much as $400,000 in annual gross income. The letter emphasized that the face peel "offers a viable alternative to the risks of surgical procedures" and referred to "our SAFE, proven system."

Walerstein came before Ron Wyden and other members of the House subcommittee on November 2, 1989. After a lengthy exchange involving Walerstein's refusal to be photographed, videotaped, or tape-recorded, testimony began. Walerstein testified that he was president of Medical Marketing Services Inc., a business that "helps physicians learn how to market the phenol-based chemical exfoliation procedure." His "trainer" for this procedure was a physician who had lost his license following an arrest for "inappropriately prescribing" drugs to an undercover policewoman.

The Mary Church affair might be seen as an example of what Jack Bierig had argued all along: that unregulated medical advertising poses an unacceptable threat to the public

Controversial. Abrasive.
A brilliant researcher. Often tactless.
The father of modern immunology.

Miles is proud to present this series on...

Powerful Innovators

Powerful Physician

Almroth Edward Wright (1861-1947)

After years of medical studies, Wright's appointment as professor of pathology at the Army Medical School in England led to his development of a typhoid fever vaccine—allowing most British troops to enter World War I immunized against this deadly infection.

Wright's dedication to the field of immunization continued with substantial help from his impressive research team, which included Alexander Fleming.

After the war, Wright's influence declined, partly because of his perceived abrasive, often tactless style. His unpopular opinions drew the attention of George Bernard Shaw, who based <u>The Doctor's Dilemma</u> on his discussions with Wright and his colleagues at St. Mary's Hospital.

His controversial theories aside, Wright's significant achievements include the development of vaccines against enteric tuberculosis, pneumonia, and typhoid fever.

Powerful Antimicrobial

Lower respiratory infections are hard enough to treat without the complications of a limited spectrum, resistant pathogens, and the underlying medical processes seen in alcoholics, immunocompromised patients, the elderly, and smokers. Cipro® helps simplify these problems by giving you the power to treat lower respiratory infections* effectively and confidently — every day. Once you have the power of Cipro® working with you, even serious lower respiratory infections start looking a little less threatening and a lot more manageable.

Powerful Numbers

Speak for themselves

2 ...*Twice-daily dosing, with Cipro®.*

5 ...*The number of indications for which Cipro® is indicated: lower respiratory infections, skin and skin structure infections, bone and joint infections, urinary tract infections, infectious diarrhea.**

96 ...*The percentage of favorable clinical response (resolution + improvement) with Cipro® in lower respiratory infections due to susceptible strains of indicated pathogens.*

(ciprofloxacin HCl)

The most potent fluoroquinolone.[1-3†]

CIPRO® SHOULD NOT BE USED IN CHILDREN, ADOLESCENTS, OR PREGNANT WOMEN.

See full prescribing information at the end of this book.

COMMITTED TO THERAPEUTIC EFFICIENCY

MILES

Miles Inc.
Pharmaceutical Division
400 Morgan Lane
West Haven, CT 06516

© March 1991, Miles Inc. Pharmaceutical Division   Printed in U.S.A.   CO9570E health and safety. Advertising, Bierig had suggested, was the symptom of a deeper rift in the medical conscience: the refocusing of professional priorities on maximizing profits, to the exclusion of patient welfare. But the FTC would say that Mary Church's death, although tragic and unjustified, was an isolated incident.

There are certainly aspects of the situation that are not characteristic of medicine at large: it involved an elective procedure out of the mainstream of normal medical care; the initial marketing was not done by physicians; and the horrible result implies a doctor quite out of touch with both his own capabilities and fundamental professional morality. Given these points, many doctors might find little with which to identify in the episode. Still, there is a classic red flag here, one that organized medicine can ignore only at its peril. It is very much the question that Beverly Merz, national editor for science and technology of *American Medical News*, posed when she spoke to me about medical advertising's trickle-down effect: "Today it's plastic surgery and diet centers, but what about tomorrow?"

Dr. Hugh Johnston was the chairman of the Oregon Board of Medical Examiners at the time of the Mary Church incident. He also viewed that travesty as a symbol of larger troubles within medicine. "The issue is broader than just cosmetic surgery," he advised the Wyden subcommittee. "The FTC, in its haste to do away with the good old boy, anticompetitive network, has gone too far, leaving the public open to misinformation and misused technology." Johnston told the subcommittee that some sort of legislative revisions were necessary so that open competition among doctors could coexist with appropriate regulation of what he called "buccaneer physicians."

Ron Wyden described the medical world since *AMA* v. *FTC* as an open zone for aggressive and often irresponsible marketing, with legitimate physicians powerless to police their own ranks. Wyden's plans now include drafting legislation that will prescribe standards of management and care in the entire area of ambulatory care—docs-in-the-boxes, urgent-care centers, and outpatient surgery clinics. "The general theme here," Steve Jenning told me, "is retrenching after the Reagan years, when organized medicine became a laissez-faire arm of the private sector. While we agree wholeheartedly with competition, we're looking for ways to ensure a modicum of consumer safety and service efficacy."

Jenning continued, "For too long, people were told you can't have both. Well, that's bullshit."

Representative Fortney "Pete" Stark (D-Calif.) wants to ban doctor-owned referral centers.

Another member of Congress who has become involved in the fracas surrounding medical profiteering is Representative Fortney "Pete" Stark, a Democrat from California. Stark is confronting the latest version of clinical commercialism: physician-owned "referral centers." X-ray and diagnostic-imaging facilities, pharmacies, medical-equipment suppliers, optical shops, fitness and swim clubs, laboratories, and centers for outpatient surgery and physical therapy have all become common investment opportunities for doctors, creating what might seem to be conflicts of interest. Pete Stark believes these are conflicts, claiming that "terrible overutilization and waste occur" when doctors refer patients to businesses they own or have an interest in.

The phenomenon of physician-owned subsidiary businesses is a direct result of the FTC's effort to deregulate the practice of medicine and is easily the most widespread current expression of the doctor-as-entrepreneur trend. As with other arguments on this broad issue, critics of "self-referral" are dismissed as being out of the loop, at odds with the demands of modern medicine.

The New York Times examined the matter in the summer of 1991 in an extensive special report. Journalists Robert Pear and Erik Eckholm focused on the Atlanta area, detailing the investments of several physicians in magnetic resonance imaging (MRI) centers. Atlanta-based doctors, reported Pear and Eckholm, share ownership in more than half the MRI facilities in the metropolitan area. Given the cost of acquiring even one machine, profits must run high for investors to recoup the initial investment. The opportunity for abuse in such a situation is obvious.

Yet the management firms behind MRI centers (in Atlanta and throughout the United States) make no effort to conceal their interest in creating captive markets. In one case, a company's prospectus explicitly states an intention to develop a large base of physician-investors "who will be inclined to refer their patients to an MRI facility in which they have a financial interest."

Any doctor who owns all or part of an MRI center, or any other such service, would have a rather strong motivation to send his or her patients to those outlets. From a business perspective this not only makes perfect sense—it's the whole point. From an ethical perspective, physician-owned referral services confuse and compromise proper clinical judgment. It is the same debate that has raged since the days of Sidney Garfield, in somewhat different attire.

On the surface, there seems nothing wrong with physicians owning businesses other than their practices, and it seems reasonable they would invest in medical and health-care services or supplies. But I find myself asking how and when a physician draws the line. If a patient, for example, needs a lab test (as virtually every patient does), should that patient be directed to the lab his doctor owns? When should the person not be referred? Should the patient be given a choice of three possible labs in the area (but a subtle push toward one in particular)? Or is the matter settled by simply disclosing the doctor's financial interest? Navigating such waters is a dangerous proposition for physicians, according to Dr. Arnold Relman.

Relman, widely known as the longtime editor of *The New England Journal of Medicine*, is an unreserved critic of the entire spectrum of medical commercialization. "The whole climate in medicine is becoming more commercial and competitive," he told reporters Pear and Eckholm. "It's putting doctors in situations that force them to behave like entrepreneurs to survive."

Another variation in the self-referral theme is the process of inviting doctors to invest in hospital ventures. Texas financier Richard Rainwater has been buying into the hospital-chain market, with a specific plan to bring doctors aboard as limited partners. As with the MRI arrangements, the rationale is the same—to encourage self-referral. Proponents of the approach continue to insist that it's a good idea to have physicians in the fold, where they can monitor spending patterns and help keep a hospital on its toes.

Physicians can also, however, use their partnerships to block or undermine competition, as evidenced by two recent FTC cases in which one group of physicians denied hospital privileges to physicians from a competing HMO and also attempted to leverage more profitable terms from third-party insurers. The FTC effectively put a stop to these practices, but the cases illustrate other troubling facets of self-referral beyond the concerns for conflict of interest.

Relman has observed that patients are becoming economic commodities as opposed to human beings. Echoing this is Dr. Ron Anderson, chairman of the Texas Board of Health, who said, "It stinks ethically when you see the patient as a great big pork chop coming in the front door." Meanwhile Pete Stark, as chairman of the Ways and Means health subcommittee, is moving to contain abuses of self-referral through antikickback legislation.

This legislation is designed to stop self-referral of Medicare and Medicaid patients, thereby controlling "double-dipping" at the government's expense. Responsibility for policing doctors' self-referral falls to the inspector general's office of the Department of Health and Human Services, headed by notorious "doc cop" Richard Kusserow. Kusserow's spokesman has indicated that firm steps will be taken toward prosecuting self-referral violators, but (as is characteristic of any political solution) antikickback regulations are compromised by numerous loopholes.

It is currently permissible, for example, for physicians to own up to 40 percent of a health-related business they refer patients to. And 40 percent of that business' income may permissibly be derived from the referral of patients by doctor-owners. This means the inspector general's office must investigate any suspicious joint-health-care ventures. Pete Stark would make it much simpler by imposing a ban on *all* self-referral.

Arnold Relman retired as editor of *The New England Journal* in the summer of 1991, moving on to Harvard Medical School, where he is Professor of Medicine and Social Medicine. I recently telephoned him at his office in Brigham and Women's Hospital.

"The FTC thinks medicine is just another business," he told me. "And most economists do. Very few economists understand that in health care there really cannot be a free market,

Dr. Arnold Relman, former editor of *The New England Journal of Medicine* and critic of medical commercialization, says that the profession must return to its ethical roots.

in the classical sense." The self-referral issue is simply the latest symptom, in Relman's view, of a profession undecided about its role in contemporary American culture.

"Commercialization is *the* issue," Relman said. And how it's addressed, he thinks, will determine the future of American medicine.

"I also happen to believe," Relman continued, "that the key

to solving our health-care problems in the future is in the hands of the profession. Nothing really effective or successful can happen that does not involve the active participation of physicians. You can diddle around all you want changing the insurance systems or payment systems. You can argue until the cows come home as to whether we should have a Canadian-style insurance system or one in which individuals pay according to their means. But in the last analysis, the answer to finding a cost-effective, high-quality system lies in how doctors respond to the challenge."

I noted that organized medicine had made some valiant attempts to meet the assaults on the profession, but the results seemed disparate and unbalanced.

Relman agreed, pointing out that when medicine finally gets around to sorting out what it wants to be and what role it wants to play in American society, the central question it will have to face is this: Should it continue to move in the direction of commercialization?

"I believe that the ultimate salvation of medicine—its ultimate independence and integrity—will depend on its opting for a professional ethic. At some point the profession will have to say, We are not businessmen, and we are not going to be placed in situations in which we must act like businessmen in order to survive. Because if we accept those situations, we're going to be treated like businessmen. And that means we're going to be regulated, we're going to be controlled like any other vendor. Health care will become a public utility and will be regulated as such. We'll lose our freedom to practice medicine according to our best professional judgment. We'll be told what we can do and under what circumstances. We'll be second-guessed and paperworked and administered and managed to death. The only way to avoid this state of affairs is to separate ourselves from commercial motives. We have to say that we are professionals and that we need arrangements that will enable us to act accordingly."

I observed that all the problems he mentioned were certainly with us already, adding that new arrangements have been called for by many within this most divisive of controversies. What, I asked, might be done to keep things from getting worse?

"Well," Relman said, "I'm writing my own book on that subject." But he referred again to his position that any workable solutions in medicine's conflict between patients and profits must be advanced and maintained by physicians themselves. To that end, Relman added, "the concern with medical commercialization is terribly important. The more doctors hear about it and the more they understand what the history is and what the facts are and what the issues are, the better off the profession will be."

CHAPTER SIX

COMMERCIALISM IN ACTION

aymond Gavery, M.D., is based in Gurnee, Illinois, a short drive from Chicago. He trained in internal medicine at Cook County Hospital in Chicago from 1972 to 1975 and recalls his residency as a time when that hospital was so short-handed "you just jumped in to help wherever you were needed." As an internist in private practice, he soon found himself missing those aspects of medicine he had dealt with routinely at Cook County: obstetrics, pediatrics, office gynecology. So, he said, he decided to "upgrade to family practice" and was board-certified in that area in 1979. Now 51 years old, he looks back on a clinical career filled with both "wonderful moments" and an ever-increasing confusion about the proper role of doctors in a changing society.

The advent of commercialization, Gavery believes, is a central factor in medicine's current upheaval. He refers to the profession's last 10 years as a "story of disasters, because we [physicians] never changed in response to the social changes going on all around us. We didn't understand our market, or what it expected of us. We were caught short. Our prerogatives slipped through our fingers, and we let other entities control the destiny of medicine."

The son of a physician, Gavery comes from what he terms a "very traditional, old-fashioned doctor's family." He describes his father as the quintessential representative of the older order in medicine, a man who understood that his primary responsibility in life was to his patients; for him, the term *marketplace* had no relevance. But when the younger Gavery began his medical career some 15 years ago, his father's world was already slipping into that nostalgic haze we reserve for an idealized past. Dr. Raymond Gavery recognized that, professionally speaking, he was the denizen of a brave new world.

He concluded that all of medicine's problems were related to money: Technology was proliferating at a stunning pace. The malpractice crisis constituted a kind of dry rot in doctors' relationships with their patients and with each other. Federal and private insurance systems strained under the weight of reimbursement demands. Doctors like Gavery, with small practices, began to feel the squeeze of competition and of slow or nonexistent third-party payments.

Despite medicine's burdens, Gavery managed to survive. But by the early 1980s, the hassles of dealing with the government and with insurance companies had become overwhelming. Gavery met with a variety of medical-practice consultants, "taking what I could use and throwing out the rest." Though he had built a prosperous family practice, he felt frustrated by his consultants' limited vision of private-practice medicine. In 1987, Gavery began restructuring his practice-management system on his own. Then he heard about Francorp Inc.

"It was over lunch with a friend," Gavery said. "My friend told me about having had his [nonmedical] business evaluated for franchise possibilities. He thought my ideas might be appealing and suggested I go to Francorp, where I talked to a man named Gary Kisel."

The Chicago-based Francorp, Gavery learned, was a giant in the franchising world, having assisted hundreds of businesses with both large and small franchising arrangements. Gary Kisel was its senior vice-president. "I felt rather silly at first," Gavery said. "A family-practice physician going to see a man who handled fast-food chains."

The two met in May of 1988. Kisel had been with the company for eight years and had been involved in evaluating the "franchisability" of businesses since 1985. "You name an industry and I worked with it," Kisel told me. "Hotels, lawn services, dry cleaners, pharmacies."

Dr. Raymond Gavery, whose desire for a traditional, family-oriented medical practice resulted in the American Family Doctor concept, visits one of AFD's francishees in Chicago.

What he had never dealt with, Kisel conceded, was a doctor with a freestanding medical practice.

"At the outset," Kisel said, "I was struck by the total lack of understanding of business among doctors. An outsider might imagine, since there's always been a tradition of private practice in this country, that doctors are pretty good business people. Not so." On the other hand, Kisel admitted, he didn't know much about doctors—what they thought about or what they wanted. So Gavery and Kisel each began to learn about the other's world.

Gavery maintained that medicine's professional ethics would be revived and public respect would be restored if doctors could once again practice a patient-oriented medicine free from intrusion by insurance companies and the federal government, and from the myriad problems involved in simply conducting business in modern America. So, using his own practice as a prototype, Gavery drew up for Kisel an idealistic and ambitious blueprint for the restoration of a traditional medical practice. He proposed a system of work-to-own, fee-for-service practices in which the physician-owners would be committed to their neighborhoods and communities in a manner rarely seen in American medicine today. This would be possible, Gavery explained, only if the physicians were somehow freed from the administrative aspects of practice, such as personnel management, accounting, staff training, bill collecting, and so forth. If physicians could regain their personal stake in their practices, Gavery added, they could once again realize the emotional rewards that come with the practice of medicine.

In September 1988, after four months of research on the feasibility of Gavery's vision, Kisel agreed to take the doctor as a client. Kisel began his project development with some basic questions about the "target audience," quickly learning that such terminology was foreign to his new client. So he introduced Raymond Gavery to some of the essentials of business marketing: demographics, site evaluation, advertising, and promotion. Thus began a physician-initiated practice-management alternative that included not only a reasonable sense of marketplace but an intrinsic concern for patient and physician welfare.

In the course of developing Gavery's ideas into a fully franchisable business concept, Kisel proposed that the enterprise have a trademark.

"I was told I had to have a recognizable logo," Gavery says. "It was then I began to feel truly commercialized, and it didn't feel right. You know—in order to make my ideas work, I needed a big plastic trademark?"

Absolutely, advised Gary Kisel. Like it or not, the consumer-patient has been conditioned to accept "chain services," which promise equal quality and known quantity from one location to another. Kisel said it would be counterproductive—hopeless, in fact—to deny this fact of life. Why not take advantage of it?

The brand name they came up with was American Family Doctor. At the outset, Gavery was uncomfortable. "It's like 'Pearle Vision,'" he told me. His ethics ran against making himself a product, but he has since become reconciled. The inescapable fact, he observed, is that it worked. "A brand name, the idea of opening in shopping centers—all this bothered me a great deal. But the public is taking to it." Gavery believes other physicians must accept what he has had to accept. "Doctors have to acknowledge that their patients are conditioned toward known names and known systems."

So the working plan for American Family Doctor (AFD) came into focus: multiple sites, recognizable signs, convenient locations and hours, and sophisticated marketing and advertising—including telemarketing and direct mail. To this was added comprehensive management assistance and expertise. AFD not only assists the physician-owners with computerized accounting, coding, patient-management, and utilization-review systems but also consults with them on office design, site selection, equipment purchases, staff recruitment and training, billing, and collections. The franchise even helps with a grand-opening party. In return, the physicians in the solo or small-group practices pay AFD 8½ percent of their collectibles. The cost of a franchise is an affordable $35,000, and young physicians build equity in their practices over the course of a few years.

Gavery and Kisel feel that their system is the best possible marriage of modern commerce and medical values. The point, Kisel told me, is to assure quality and all-round satisfaction by helping doctors own fee-for-service practices, allowing them to establish long-term relationships with their communities.

"We want to bring back what America feels it has lost in

Powerful Innovators

Next to excellence is the appreciation of it.

William Makepeace Thackeray

Miles is pleased to sponsor this series on Powerful Innovators to remember, recognize, and appreciate the truly remarkable achievements of the best of the medical profession.

We salute these individuals; we applaud their efforts; we remember their deeds.

More importantly, we salute and applaud the efforts today's physicians make every day.

H. Brian Allen, MD, FFPM
Director, Scientific Relations
Miles Inc.
Pharmaceutical Division

Powerful Numbers

Speak for themselves

*1 ... The number of **fluoroquinolones** indicated for lower respiratory infections, skin and skin structure infections, bone and joint infections, urinary tract infections, infectious diarrhea.**

96 ... The percentage of favorable clinical response (resolution + improvement) with Cipro® in lower respiratory infections due to susceptible strains of indicated pathogens.

13,000,000 ... The estimated number of patients treated to date with Cipro® in this country.†

Cipro® TABLETS

(ciprofloxacin HCl)

The most potent fluoroquinolone.[1-3‡]

CIPRO® SHOULD NOT BE USED IN CHILDREN, ADOLESCENTS, OR PREGNANT WOMEN.

* Due to susceptible strains of indicated pathogens. See indicated organisms in prescribing information.

† Estimate based on prescription data from IMS, *National Prescription Audit,* and PDS, *U.S. Hospital Drug and Diagnosis Audit,* October 1987 through June 1990.

‡ In vitro activity does not necessarily imply a correlation with in vivo results.

See full prescribing information at the end of this book.

COMMITTED TO THERAPEUTIC EFFICIENCY

MILES

Miles Inc.
Pharmaceutical Division
400 Morgan Lane
West Haven, CT 06516

medical care but make it economically feasible," explained Kisel. "The public has just about had it with the medical-industrial complex. Long waits, rude staff—and then the doc is too tired or too burned out or just too uninterested to listen. And why not? He or she is no more than an employee, with no emotional or financial investment, no equity. We're trying to offer an alternative."

In emphasizing this point, Gavery told me he thinks the charges of banditry and greed that are often leveled at physicians stem from the chaos imposed by federal government regulations. Physicians, he contended, have shown an inability to stand up to bureaucrats and politicians. So, for that matter, has the AMA.

"The AMA seems to be doing its best," Gavery said. But he finds the AMA's practice seminars and pamphlets on management to be finger-in-the-dike strategies. Instead, Gavery and Kisel propose a comprehensive interplay between medicine and business, with primary-care physicians repositioned in full-service practices, as opposed to being one-visit providers of urgent care. Backed by modern financial and management techniques, American medicine will be back on track. Doctors, Gavery predicted, "will follow their consciences" and revive both the public image of their profession and its cost-effectiveness.

There are currently two American Family Doctor sites in operation, one in St. Charles, Illinois, a booming western suburb of Chicago, where internist Mark Lewis has borrowed the capital to purchase the franchise for the area. The other site is in Chicago proper, on North Clybourn Avenue. It wasn't long ago that "no doctor would set foot in this part of town," according to Dr. Armand Gonzalzles, one of three physicians working to own the practice. Now undergoing gentrification, the neighborhood is a pastiche of down-and-dirty industrial ruins, warehouses, and condemned tenements along with video rental shops, cheery cafes, and the bright little strip shopping center in which American Family Doctor prominently occupies one end.

Gonzalzles is a pediatrician, probably one of the few physicians in this country practicing in the neighborhood where he

Freed from paperwork by AFD's system, pediatrician Armand Gonzalzles had time for Halloween last year. Here, dressed as Father Time, he sees a patient in his Chicago office.

grew up. He joined American Family Doctor in February 1991, bringing an established clientele along with him and assuring the new outlet a patient base. For him, the move was an auspicious one.

"I was getting killed by management problems," he said. "Buried in paper. Spending what profit I made moving that paper."

What about the shopping-center environment of American Family Doctor? Gonzalzles shrugged. "It doesn't matter. It may be a little strange at first, but look: I'm me, doing what I do. It just happens to be in this building."

I told Gonzalzles that some other physicians to whom I'd spoken had expressed reservations about AFD's telemarketing and direct-mail-advertising push. He waved a hand, laughing. "It's okay for the hospitals, but not for us docs? Come on. What AFD's doing is lightweight by comparison. Besides, all that's really happening is that information is being disseminated. You know—we're here, we're available." He laughed again. "This is advertising that's really in the best tradition of the AMA hard-liners: an announcement. No solicitation, no pressure."

Gonzalzles leaned forward in his chair. "Listen," he said, "the way you build a practice is the way you've always built a practice: by treating people well, with respect. You smile at them when they come in, you recognize them and remember their names, you're open and honest with them. And you deliver first-rate medical care. There's nothing in the AFD idea that stops any of that from happening. If anything, it makes it easier."

One of Gonzalzles' associates on North Clybourn is Mitchell Carneol, an internist, who showed me around the AFD facility. In line with Raymond Gavery's original vision, it is well-lighted and cheerful, the walkways neatly engineered to steer patients through clinical areas and out to the billing desk. As we strolled about, Carneol spoke about the financial pressures on a young physician that make buying an AFD franchise an attractive option.

"It's difficult to go into practice for yourself these days," Carneol said. "If you're not invited into a well-established group, what can you do? The days are over when a doc can walk into a bank and say, I'm Doctor So-and-So and I want to open up down the street and how about it?" We made our way back to Carneol's office. "So I heard about AFD," he continued, "and it sounded like a foot in the door."

I asked about the elaborate managerial support systems Gavery and Kisel spoke of and about how much of his time is involved with overseeing operations like billing, accounting, and payroll. "Very little," Carneol said. "That's the beauty of the idea. It seems like this is the way it used to be for doctors. Your focus is on your patients—the job you were trained to do."

Yet how, in the end, is the American Family Doctor concept truly different from the docs-in-the-boxes and urgent-care centers mushrooming on street corners all across the country? Granted, AFD sites will (ideally) be doctor-owned. But it takes no special reach of the imagination to envision abuses of American Family Doctor, abuses that would spring from the concept's potential to be operated as a large-scale business and not as a group of privately owned medical practices.

What, for example, might stop a nonphysician investor from exerting control of an AFD site through fiscal manipulation? Nothing I can see in the idea precludes such "silent partner" interference. What happens when working-to-own doctors don't share Gavery's vision and lose interest, or leave town, or default on loans for one reason or another? The AFD outlet's ownership would revert to the original investor—a situation that would be no different from the corporate owners of docs-in-the-boxes.

Then there's the interesting problem of AFD outlets *looking* precisely like the kind of family-practice and urgent-care satellite clinics usually owned and operated by hospital chains and HMOs. If AFD's version of such storefront and shopping-mall clinics aims to be different, the franchise needs to demonstrate in practical terms exactly *how* they will be different. There is nothing in the physical aspects of an AFD site that immediately communicates the franchise owner's presumed commitment to high-quality service and loyalty to a patient population, nothing to distinguish it from its medical competitors on other street corners.

Another troubling aspect of the American Family Doctor concept is that of "relieving" physicians of the burdens of conducting business. Admittedly, the hassle factor in medicine is a major issue for doctors, as Armand Gonzalzles pointed out. But to separate physicians from the realities of modern business altogether is ultimately shortsighted. It simply continues the current trend toward centralizing the financial control of medicine in the worlds of business and politics. If physicians wish to wield more power in their working lives, they must learn to function as business people *and* clinicians rather than continuing to avoid business concerns as somehow beneath them or beyond their ken.

In our conversations, Raymond Gavery spoke repeatedly to me about values like integrity, loyalty, and self-esteem, advancing the theory that physicians might be able to express such qualities through a commodity system, thereby overriding the trivializing effects of that system on their work as professionals. The question before Gavery and American Family Doctor, then, is an intriguing one: Can the demands of hard-bitten competition be used to foster a rebirth of the American physician's soul?

Perhaps, provided that all the business variables fall into place each and every time and that participating physicians subscribe completely to Raymond Gavery's vision. American Family Doctor remains an early experiment in the fusion of medicine and commerce; only time will tell us whether it will work across the board, for many doctors and in many cities. Until then, Dr. Raymond Gavery's franchised medicine represents (with a caveat) a promising alternative to young physicians looking for fee-for-service private practice in towns where they're needed.

CHAPTER SEVEN

FUTURE IMPERFECT

he FTC predicted that commercializing medicine would help to relieve the problems of spiraling cost and mediocre service by allowing the rules of the marketplace to prevail. The AMA predicted that deregulating physician advertising would provoke a damaging onslaught of fraudulent advertising that would discredit the profession and endanger an unwitting public.

Neither of those predictions has proved true. On the one hand, we have seen no particular improvement in the way we deliver health care since 1982. If anything, medicine is mired more deeply than ever in an expensive, bureaucratized, and indifferent system of service delivery. On the other hand, though advertising itself has become common, phony advertising has not.

The FTC and the AMA both held fundamentally accurate, though very different, views about the practice of medicine in the United States. The FTC was right in its contention that the AMA had no ground for insisting it was a nonprofit organization not subject to the laws governing restraint of trade. The AMA's nonprofit status had been compromised as early as the mid-1970s by revelations that it used the profits from the huge advertising revenues earned by its publications to buy political influence. And the association, whose own Judicial Council had a longstanding rule that it was unethical for physicians to buy stock in drug companies, was also chastised for investing its members' retirement funds in drug companies, a conflict of interest that led journalists Morton Mintz and Jerry Cohen, the authors of *Power, Inc.*, to describe the AMA of the period as suffering from "ethical myopia."

But the AMA was right when it warned that many routinely accepted techniques of business and commerce are inappropriate to medical practice. Yes, medicine is a marketplace—but it is not a typical one. True, there is a product—but it is not quite like shoes or hamburgers or automobiles.

These conflicts were never really resolved. Although attorneys on both sides of *AMA* v. *FTC* today attest that they made every attempt to settle the case, it is clear that the idea of compromise did not figure in anyone's plans. Judge Barnes wonders why the AMA "didn't just accept a consent order." Jack Bierig replies that any consent order drafted by Barnes would have been nothing more than a one-sided settlement that met FTC objectives, and he muses on the agency's "arbitrariness" and Judge Barnes's "blinders." It seems that at the time, neither the AMA nor the FTC could see its way clear to move toward the center, to reach an agreement of proportion and balance.

What we have inherited from *AMA* v. *FTC*, therefore, is one of the central problems for medicine today: there is no policy at all regarding commercialization. The AMA (and the medical community in general) lurched away from the FTC's victory completely unprepared for the deregulated environment that awaited. The result has been a whirling free fall of marketing, the great buying and selling of American medicine. We have doctors who are drug repackagers and limited partners in you-name-it health-related enterprises. There are medical infomercials, ever-bolder ads in newspapers and magazines, ads on roadside billboards, ads on the sides of city buses. A New York City ob-gyn advertises fertility services for "when everything else has failed." A dermatologist in San Francisco markets her own brand of cosmetics—and provides logo-imprinted shopping bags for carrying the purchases away.

One of the casualties of this process, oddly enough, has been primary care. Although commercialization per se may not be the bogeyman that some would have physicians believe, commercialization carried to such extremes and combined with the lure of glamour medicine misleads and distracts both the profession and the public from what 90 percent of medicine is really about—providing basic primary care for all Americans, many of whom are poor, nonwhite, uninsured, and uneducated. Primary-care residency programs are not filled in many medical schools, and new medical graduates are ever more frequently attracted to what Dr. Thomas Krizek, Maurice Goldblatt Distinguished Service Professor of Surgery at the University of Chicago, calls "controlled lifestyle specialties." These include plastic surgery and certain branches of ophthalmology and dermatology—the very specialties whose services can effectively be sold to the affluent.

This waning of interest in the frontline aspects of medicine is a peculiar side effect of commercialism, because marketing and competition may actually be used to their best effect in primary care. Despite the popular notion that primary care represents the mundane side of medicine, it is also the base of the profession's organizational pyramid. Although direct patient self-referral to specialists has been on the rise, mainstream medicine still depends on primary care to act as the gateway to its extensive superstructure of specialists and subspecialists.

In fact, primary care has the potential to lead medicine toward a more rational use of sensible marketing and business techniques tailored specifically for physicians and other health-care providers. Commercial tools like educational newsletters, questionnaires, and informative mailings will in no way degrade the doctor-patient relationship. If they work— that is if they produce a better-informed patient who has more confidence in his physician—they may even demonstrate to medicine at large how advertising, as long as it avoids overkill or unnecessary hype, can be used without compromising the profession's dignity and traditional ethical concerns. Dr. Raymond Gavery's American Family Doctor represents a laudable first attempt in the trend toward an organized, dignified approach to selling clinical skills to people who need general medical services.

Before such an approach is embraced by the profession as a whole, however, physicians and the American Medical Association must call for more substantial research on medical commercialization. When I began work on this book, I requested a computer search from the National Library of Medicine's database for references pertinent to my subject. I expected to be inundated with paper. Instead I received a 13-page printout that represented all the salient research done in the area of medical commercialism and physician advertising in the last 16 years. Only a few of the 74 citations actually analyzed the effects of commerce and advertising on physicians and patients.

Perhaps because of this lack of research, doctors as a group are generally uninformed about both the history of the profession's rising commercialism and the effects that the phenomenon will have on the essential nature of the profession. Some physicians to whom I spoke while researching this book were surprised and rather mystified by its subject matter. The subjects of medical advertising and the ethics of patient solicitation seemed like foreign territory to many of them, uncomfortable issues best avoided in polite medical company. Such reactions stem from ignorance and the persistent, hidebound image of the physician as a professional who is beyond the influence of commerce.

Nothing is further from the truth, and doctors can ill afford to pretend otherwise. Commercialism is a fact of life; physicians who do not control it will be controlled by it. Simply put, medicine must find a way to retain its status as a profession while reaping the benefits of commercialism.

How can this be accomplished?

First, the medical student's basic education in ethics must consider the issues of advertising and marketing in light of the principal arguments that have divided the profession for more than 40 years. Today's students, steeped in a commercial environment since birth, must learn to question their assumptions—or lack of them—in the context of the profession's ethical concerns.

Second, medical-school curricula should include introductory courses in marketing. Being comfortable in a commercial environment is not the same thing as being able to manage it, and sending new physicians out to practice without this knowledge has become untenable. Most practicing physicians (particularly those in the early stages of their careers) know little about such matters as the demographics of their

The University of Chicago's Dr. Thomas Krizek, a plastic surgeon, says, "Medicine has become an industry, which is a terrible thing to have happened in my lifetime."

clientele or how to assess and cater to its needs. The native distrust most doctors have of business tools such as these should be countered early with courses addressing the reality of the commercial environment and strategies physicians can use to survive without compromising their professional principles.

Third, physician advertising must be seen as an opportunity for medicine and its practitioners to redefine a professional identity. Although such advertising will always have its cowboys and cowgirls, its clever misleaders and errant souls, medical marketing is not by definition a haven for bad actors. In fact, it offers the profession a rare opportunity to shore up its foundations and remember its fundamental purpose: taking care of patients.

The day is long past when physicians could comfortably ignore the social and economic contexts of medical practice, a point made by Dr. Julia Reade and Dr. Richard Ratzan in *The New England Journal of Medicine* when they wrote, "Members of the medical profession have a collective moral responsibility to address these concerns and to force themselves to make the necessary difficult choices. We must face the realization that not only does the public suffer from inconsistent applications and definitions of standards, but ultimately our professional credibility is at stake."

This responsibility includes the continuing obligation of doctors to closely monitor the ethical implications of their behavior. Medicine, notes Thomas Krizek, once shared with the ministry and the law a sense of calling, "and a calling is different from a job. The standards to which these professions were held and to which they held themselves were different from those associated with jobs. Those who would have us swim in the same waters as, say, car dealers will find they can't have it both ways."

Commercial or not, modern medicine's basic operational contract is what it has always been: the doctor-patient relationship. This relationship, the fundamental factor in health care, has clearly suffered (and not only from commercialization), yet it remains the hallmark of the art of medicine. This is the common ground that unites physicians, the source of medicine's best interests and finest directions. It is the standard against which everything else must be measured.

ADDITIONAL COPIES

To order copies of *Medicine For Sale* for friends or colleagues, please write to The Grand Rounds Press, Whittle Books, 333 Main Ave., Knoxville, Tenn. 37902. Please include the recipient's name, mailing address, and, where applicable, primary specialty and ME number.

For a single copy, please enclose a check for $21.95 plus $1.50 for postage and handling, payable to The Grand Rounds Press. Quantities may be limited. Discounts apply to bulk orders when available. For more information about The Grand Rounds Press, please call 800-765-5889.

Also available, at the same price, are copies of the previous books from The Grand Rounds Press:
The Doctor Watchers by Spencer Vibbert
The New Genetics by Leon Jaroff
Surgeon Koop by Gregg Easterbrook
Inside Medical Washington by James H. Sammons, M.D.

Please allow four weeks for delivery.
Tennessee residents must add 7¾ percent sales tax.

PRESCRIBING INFORMATION
APPENDIX

CIPRO®

(ciprofloxacin hydrochloride) TABLETS

MILES

PZ100735

DESCRIPTION

Cipro® (ciprofloxacin hydrochloride) is a synthetic broad spectrum antibacterial agent for oral administration. Ciprofloxacin, a fluoroquinolone, is available as the monohydrochloride monohydrate salt of 1-cyclopropyl-6-fluoro-1, 4-dihydro-4-oxo-7-(1-piperazinyl)-3-quinolinecarboxylic acid. It is a faintly yellowish to light yellow crystalline substance with a molecular weight of 385.8. Its empirical formula is $C_{17}H_{18}FN_3O_3 \cdot HCl \cdot H_2O$ and its chemical structure is as follows:

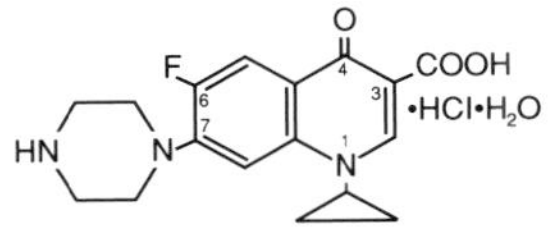

Cipro® is available in 250-mg, 500-mg and 750-mg (ciprofloxacin equivalent) film-coated tablets. The inactive ingredients are starch, microcrystalline cellulose, silicon dioxide, crospovidone, magnesium stearate, hydroxypropyl methylcellulose, titanium dioxide, polyethylene glycol and water. Ciprofloxacin differs from other quinolones in that it has a fluorine atom at the 6-position, a piperazine moiety at the 7-position, and a cyclopropyl ring at the 1-position. Examples of other antibacterial drugs in the quinolone class are nalidixic acid, cinoxacin, and norfloxacin.

CLINICAL PHARMACOLOGY

Cipro® tablets are rapidly and well absorbed from the gastrointestinal tract after oral administration. The absolute bioavailability is approximately 70% with no substantial loss by first pass metabolism. Serum concentrations increase proportionately with the dose as shown:

Dose (mg)	Maximum Serum Concentration (mcg/mL)	Area Under Curve (AUC) (mcg • hr/mL)
250	1.2	4.8
500	2.4	11.6
750	4.3	20.2
1000	5.4	30.8

Maximum serum concentrations are attained 1 to 2 hours after oral dosing. Mean concentrations 12 hours after dosing with 250, 500, or 750 mg are 0.1, 0.2, and 0.4 mcg/mL, respectively. The serum elimination half-life in subjects with normal renal function is approximately 4 hours.

Approximately 40 to 50% of an orally administered dose is excreted in the urine as unchanged drug. After a 250-mg oral dose, urine concentrations of ciprofloxacin usually exceed 200 mcg/mL during the first two hours and are approximately 30 mcg/mL at 8 to 12 hours after dosing. The urinary excretion of ciprofloxacin is virtually complete within 24 hours after dosing. The renal clearance of ciprofloxacin, which is approximately 300 mL/minute, exceeds the normal glomerular filtration rate of 120 mL/minute. Thus, active tubular secretion would seem to play a significant role in its elimination. Co-administration of probenecid with ciprofloxacin results in about a 50% reduction in the ciprofloxacin renal clearance and a 50% increase in its concentration in the systemic circulation. Although bile concentrations of ciprofloxacin are several fold higher than serum concentrations after oral dosing, only a small amount of the dose administered is recovered from the bile as unchanged drug. An additional 1-2% of the dose is recovered from the bile in the form of metabolites. Approximately 20 to 35% of an oral dose is recovered from the feces within 5 days after dosing. This may arise from either biliary clearance or transintestinal elimination. Four metabolites have been identified in human urine which together account for approximately 15% of an oral dose. The metabolites have antimicrobial activity, but are less active than unchanged ciprofloxacin.

When Cipro® is given concomitantly with food, there is a delay in the absorption of the drug, resulting in peak concentrations that are closer to 2 hours after dosing rather than 1 hour. The overall absorption, however, is not substantially affected. Concurrent administration of antacids containing magnesium hydroxide or aluminum hydroxide may reduce the bioavailability of ciprofloxacin by as much as 90% (See Precautions).

Concomitant administration of ciprofloxacin with theophylline decreases the clearance of theophylline resulting in elevated serum theophylline levels, and increased risk of a patient developing CNS or other adverse reactions (See Precautions).

In patients with reduced renal function, the half-life of ciprofloxacin is slightly prolonged. Dosage adjustments may be required (See Dosage and Administration).

In preliminary studies in patients with stable chronic liver cirrhosis, no significant changes in ciprofloxacin pharmacokinetics have been observed. The kinetics of ciprofloxacin in patients with acute hepatic insufficiency, however, have not been fully elucidated.

The binding of ciprofloxacin to serum proteins is 20 to 40% which is not likely to be high enough to cause significant protein binding interactions with other drugs.

After oral administration ciprofloxacin is widely distributed throughout the body. Tissue concentrations often exceed serum concentrations in both men and women, particularly in genital tissue including the prostate. Ciprofloxacin is present in active form in the saliva, nasal and bronchial secretions, sputum, skin blister fluid, lymph, peritoneal fluid, bile and prostatic secretions. Ciprofloxacin has also been detected in lung, skin, fat, muscle, cartilage, and bone. The drug diffuses into the cerebrospinal fluid (CSF); however, CSF concentrations are generally less than 10% of peak serum concentrations. Low levels of the drug have been detected in the aqueous and vitreous humors of the eye.

Microbiology: Ciprofloxacin has *in vitro* activity against a wide range of gram-negative and gram-positive organisms. The bactericidal action of ciprofloxacin results from interference with the enzyme DNA gyrase which is needed for the synthesis of bacterial DNA.

While *in vitro* studies have demonstrated the susceptibility of most strains of the following microorganisms, clinical efficacy for infections other than those included in the Indications and Usage Section has not been documented:

Gram-Negative: *Escherichia coli; Klebsiella pneumoniae; Klebsiella oxytoca; Enterobacter aerogenes; Enterobacter cloacae; Citrobacter diversus; Citrobacter freundii; Edwardsiella tarda; Salmonella enteritidis; Salmonella typhi; Shigella sonnei; Shigella flexneri; Proteus mirabilis; Proteus vulgaris; Providencia stuartii; Providencia rettgeri; Morganella morganii; Serratia marcescens; Yersinia enterocolitica; Pseudomonas aeruginosa; Acinetobacter calcoaceticus* subsp. *lwoffi; Acinetobacter calcoaceticus* subsp. *anitratus; Haemophilus influenzae; Haemophilus parainfluenzae; Haemophilus ducreyi; Neisseria gonorrhoeae; Neisseria meningitidis; Moraxella (Branhamella) catarrhalis; Campylobacter jejuni; Campylobacter coli; Aeromonas hydrophila; Aeromonas caviae; Vibrio cholerae; Vibrio parahaemolyticus; Vibrio vulnificus; Brucella melitensis; Pasteurella multocida; Legionella pneumophila.*

Gram-Positive: *Staphylococcus aureus* (including methicillin-susceptible and methicillin-resistant strains); *Staphylococcus epidermidis; Staphylococcus haemolyticus; Staphylococcus hominis; Staphylococcus saprophyticus; Streptococcus pyogenes; Streptococcus pneumoniae.*

Most strains of streptococci including *Streptococcus faecalis* are only moderately susceptible to ciprofloxacin as are *Mycobacterium tuberculosis* and *Chlamydia trachomatis.*

Most strains of *Pseudomonas cepacia* and some strains of *Pseudomonas maltophilia* are resistant to ciprofloxacin as are most anaerobic bacteria, including *Bacteroides fragilis* and *Clostridium difficile.*

Ciprofloxacin is slightly less active when tested at acidic pH. The inoculum size has little effect when tested *in vitro.* The minimum bactericidal concentration (MBC) generally does not exceed the minimum inhibitory concentration (MIC) by more than a factor of 2. Resistance to ciprofloxacin *in vitro* develops slowly (multiple-step mutation). Rapid one-step development of resistance has not been observed.

Ciprofloxacin does not cross-react with other antimicrobial agents such as beta-lactams or aminoglycosides; therefore, organisms resistant to these drugs may be susceptible to ciprofloxacin.

In vitro studies have shown that additive activity often results when ciprofloxacin is combined with other antimicrobial agents such as beta-lactams, aminoglycosides, clindamycin, or metronidazole; antagonism is observed only rarely.

Susceptibility Tests

Diffusion Techniques: Quantitative methods that require measurement of zone diameters give the most precise estimates of antibiotic susceptibility. One such procedure recommended for use with the 5-mcg ciprofloxacin disk is the National Committee for Clinical Laboratory Standards (NCCLS) approved procedure. Only a 5-mcg ciprofloxacin disk should be used, and it should not be used for testing susceptibility to less active quinolones; there are no suitable surrogate disks.

Results of laboratory tests using 5-mcg ciprofloxacin disks should be interpreted using the following criteria:

Zone Diameter (mm)	Interpretation
≥ 21	(S) Susceptible
16 – 20	(I) Intermediate (Moderately Susceptible)
≤ 15	(R) Resistant

Dilution Techniques: Broth and agar dilution methods, such as those recommended by the NCCLS, may be used to determine the minimum inhibitory concentration (MIC) of ciprofloxacin. MIC test results should be interpreted according to the following criteria:

MIC (mcg/mL)	Interpretation
≤ 1	(S) Susceptible
> 1 – ≤ 2	(I) Intermediate (Moderately Susceptible)
> 2	(R) Resistant

For any susceptibility test, a report of "susceptible" indicates that the pathogen is likely to respond to ciprofloxacin therapy. A report of "resistant" indicates that the pathogen is not likely to respond. A report of "intermediate" (moderately susceptible) indicates that the pathogen is expected to be susceptible to ciprofloxacin if high doses are used, or if the infection is confined to tissues and fluids in which high ciprofloxacin levels are obtained.

The Quality Control strains should have the following assigned daily ranges for ciprofloxacin.

QC Strains	Disk Zone Diameter (mm)	MIC (mcg/mL)
S. aureus (ATCC 25923)	22 – 30	
S. aureus (ATCC 29213)		0.25 – 1.0
E. coli (ATCC 25922)	30 – 40	0.008 – 0.03
P. aeruginosa (ATCC 27853)	25 – 33	0.25 – 1.0

INDICATIONS AND USAGE

Cipro® is indicated for the treatment of infections caused by susceptible strains of the designated microorganisms in the conditions listed below:

Lower Respiratory Infections caused by *Escherichia coli, Klebsiella pneumoniae, Enterobacter cloacae, Proteus mirabilis, Pseudomonas aeruginosa, Haemophilus influenzae, Haemophilus parainfluenzae,* and *Streptococcus pneumoniae.*

Skin and Skin Structure Infections caused by *Escherichia coli, Klebsiella pneumoniae, Enterobacter cloacae, Proteus mirabilis, Proteus vulgaris, Providencia stuartii, Morganella morganii, Citrobacter freundii, Pseudomonas aeruginosa, Staphylococcus aureus, Staphylococcus epidermidis,* and *Streptococcus pyogenes.*

Bone and Joint Infections caused by *Enterobacter cloacae, Serratia marcescens,* and *Pseudomonas aeruginosa.*

Urinary Tract Infections caused by *Escherichia coli, Klebsiella pneumoniae, Enterobacter cloacae, Serratia marcescens, Proteus mirabilis, Providencia rettgeri, Morganella morganii, Citrobacter diversus, Citrobacter freundii, Pseudomonas aeruginosa, Staphylococcus epidermidis,* and *Streptococcus faecalis.*

Infectious Diarrhea caused by *Escherichia coli* (enterotoxigenic strains), *Campylobacter jejuni, Shigella flexneri** and *Shigella sonnei** when antibacterial therapy is indicated.

*Efficacy for this organism in this organ system was studied in fewer than 10 infections.

Appropriate culture and susceptibility tests should be performed before treatment in order to isolate and identify organisms causing infection and to determine their susceptibility to ciprofloxacin. Therapy with Cipro® may be initiated before results of these tests are known; once results become available appropriate therapy should be continued. As with other drugs, some strains of *Pseudomonas aeruginosa* may develop resistance fairly rapidly during treatment with ciprofloxacin. Culture and susceptibility testing performed periodically during therapy will provide information not only on the therapeutic effect of the antimicrobial agent but also on the possible emergence of bacterial resistance.

CONTRAINDICATIONS

A history of hypersensitivity to ciprofloxacin is a contraindication to its use. A history of hypersensitivity to other quinolones may also contraindicate the use of ciprofloxacin.

WARNINGS

THE SAFETY AND EFFECTIVENESS OF CIPROFLOXACIN IN CHILDREN, ADOLESCENTS (LESS THAN 18 YEARS OF AGE), PREGNANT WOMEN, AND LACTATING WOMEN HAVE NOT BEEN ESTABLISHED. (SEE PRECAUTIONS-PEDIATRIC USE, PREGNANCY AND NURSING MOTHERS SUBSECTIONS.) Ciprofloxacin causes lameness in immature dogs. Histopathological examination of the weight-bearing joints of these dogs revealed permanent lesions of the cartilage. Related quinolone-class drugs also produce erosions of cartilage of weight-bearing joints and other signs of arthropathy in immature animals of various species. (See ANIMAL PHARMACOLOGY.)

Convulsions have been reported in patients receiving ciprofloxacin. Convulsions, increased intracranial pressure, and toxic psychosis have been reported in patients receiving ciprofloxacin and other drugs of this class. Quinolones may also cause central nervous system (CNS) stimulation which may lead to tremors, restlessness, lightheadedness, confusion and hallucinations. If these reactions occur in patients receiving ciprofloxacin, the drug should be discontinued and appropriate measures instituted. As with all quinolones, ciprofloxacin should be used with caution in patients with known or suspected CNS disorders, such as severe cerebral arteriosclerosis, epilepsy, and other factors that predispose to seizures. (See ADVERSE REACTIONS.)

SERIOUS AND FATAL REACTIONS HAVE BEEN REPORTED IN PATIENTS RECEIVING CONCURRENT ADMINISTRATION OF CIPROFLOXACIN AND THEOPHYLLINE. These reactions have included cardiac arrest, seizure, status epilepticus and respiratory failure. Although similar serious adverse events have been reported in patients receiving theophylline alone, the possibility that these reactions may be potentiated by ciprofloxacin cannot be eliminated. If concomitant use cannot be avoided, serum levels of theophylline should be monitored and dosage adjustments made as appropriate.

Serious and occasionally fatal hypersensitivity (anaphylactic) reactions, some following the first dose, have been reported in patients receiving quinolone therapy. Some reactions were accompanied by cardiovascular collapse, loss of consciousness, tingling, pharyngeal or facial edema, dyspnea, urticaria, and itching. Only a few patients had a history of hypersensitivity reactions. Serious anaphylactic reactions require immediate emergency treatment with epinephrine and other resuscitation measures, including oxygen, intravenous antihistamines, corticosteroids, pressor amines and airway management, as clinically indicated.

Severe hypersensitivity reactions characterized by rash, fever, eosinophilia, jaundice, and hepatic necrosis with fatal outcome have also been reported extremely rarely in patients receiving ciprofloxacin along with other drugs. The possibility that these reactions were related to ciprofloxacin cannot be excluded. Ciprofloxacin should be discontinued at the first appearance of a skin rash or any other sign of hypersensitivity.

Pseudomembranous colitis has been reported with nearly all antibacterial agents, including ciprofloxacin, and may range in severity from mild to life-threatening. Therefore, it is important to consider this diagnosis in patients who present with diarrhea subsequent to the administration of antibacterial agents.

Treatment with antibacterial agents alters the normal flora of the colon and may permit overgrowth of clostridia. Studies indicate that a toxin produced by *Clostridium difficile* is one primary cause of "antibiotic-associated colitis".

After the diagnosis of pseudomembranous colitis has been established, therapeutic measures should be initiated. Mild cases of pseudomembranous colitis usually respond to drug discontinuation alone. In moderate to severe cases, consideration should be given to management with fluids and electrolytes, protein supplementation and treatment with an antibacterial drug effective against *C. difficile*.

PRECAUTIONS

General: Crystals of ciprofloxacin have been observed rarely in the urine of human subjects but more frequently in the urine of laboratory animals, which is usually alkaline. (See ANIMAL PHARMACOLOGY.) Crystalluria related to ciprofloxacin has been reported only rarely in humans because human urine is usually acidic. Alkalinity of the urine should be avoided in patients receiving ciprofloxacin. Patients should be well hydrated to prevent the formation of highly concentrated urine.

Alteration of the dosage regimen is necessary for patients with impairment of renal function. (See DOSAGE AND ADMINISTRATION.)

Moderate to severe phototoxicity manifested by an exaggerated sunburn reaction has been observed in some patients who were exposed to direct sunlight while receiving some members of the quinolone class of drugs. Excessive sunlight should be avoided.

As with any potent drug, periodic assessment of organ system functions, including renal, hepatic, and hematopoietic, is advisable during prolonged therapy.

Information for Patients: Patients should be advised that ciprofloxacin may be taken with or without meals. The preferred time of dosing is two hours after a meal. Patients should also be advised to drink fluids liberally and not take antacids containing magnesium, aluminum, or calcium, products containing iron, or multivitamins containing zinc. However, usual dietary intake of calcium has not been shown to alter the absorption of ciprofloxacin.

Patients should be advised that ciprofloxacin may be associated with hypersensitivity reactions, even following a single dose, and to discontinue the drug at the first sign of a skin rash or other allergic reaction.

Ciprofloxacin may cause dizziness and lightheadedness; therefore patients should know how they react to this drug before they operate an automobile or machinery or engage in activities requiring mental alertness or coordination.

Patients should be advised that ciprofloxacin may increase the effects of theophylline and caffeine. There is a possibility of caffeine accumulation when products containing caffeine are consumed while taking quinolones.

Drug Interactions: As with other quinolones, concurrent administration of ciprofloxacin with theophylline may lead to elevated serum concentrations of theophylline and prolongation of its elimination half-life. This may result in increased risk of theophylline-related adverse reactions. (See WARNINGS.) If concomitant use cannot be avoided, serum levels of theophylline should be monitored and dosage adjustments made as appropriate.

Some quinolones, including ciprofloxacin, have also been shown to interfere with the metabolism of caffeine. This may lead to reduced clearance of caffeine and a prolongation of its serum half-life.

Concurrent administration of ciprofloxacin with antacids containing magnesium, aluminum, or calcium; with sucralfate or divalent and trivalent cations such as iron may substantially interfere with the absorption of ciprofloxacin, resulting in serum and urine levels considerably lower than desired. To a lesser extent this effect is demonstrated with zinc-containing multivitamins. (See DOSAGE AND ADMINISTRATION for concurrent administration of these agents with ciprofloxacin.)

Some quinolones, including ciprofloxacin, have been associated with transient elevations in serum creatinine in patients receiving cyclosporine concomitantly.

Quinolones have been reported to enhance the effects of the oral anticoagulant warfarin or its derivatives. When these products are administered concomitantly, prothrombin time or other suitable coagulation tests should be closely monitored.

Probenecid interferes with renal tubular secretion of ciprofloxacin and produces an increase in the level of ciprofloxacin in the serum. This should be considered if patients are receiving both drugs concomitantly.

As with other broad spectrum antimicrobial agents, prolonged use of ciprofloxacin may result in overgrowth of nonsusceptible organisms. Repeated evaluation of the patient's condition and microbial susceptibility testing is essential. If superinfection occurs during therapy, appropriate measures should be taken.

Carcinogenesis, Mutagenesis, Impairment of Fertility: Eight *in vitro* mutagenicity tests have been conducted with ciprofloxacin and the test results are listed below:

Salmonella/Microsome Test (Negative)
E. coli DNA Repair Assay (Negative)
Mouse Lymphoma Cell Forward Mutation Assay (Positive)
Chinese Hamster V_{79} Cell HGPRT Test (Negative)
Syrian Hamster Embryo Cell Transformation Assay (Negative)
Saccharomyces cerevisiae Point Mutation Assay (Negative)
Saccharomyces cerevisiae Mitotic Crossover
    and Gene Conversion Assay (Negative)
Rat Hepatocyte DNA Repair Assay (Positive)

Thus 2 of the 8 tests were positive but results of the following 3 *in vivo* test systems gave negative results:

Rat Hepatocyte DNA Repair Assay
Micronucleus Test (Mice)
Dominant Lethal Test (Mice)

Long term carcinogenicity studies in mice and rats have been completed. After daily oral dosing for up to 2 years, there is no evidence that ciprofloxacin had any carcinogenic or tumorigenic effects in these species.

Pregnancy: Teratogenic Effects. Pregnancy Category C: Reproduction studies have been performed in rats and mice at doses up to 6 times the usual daily human dose and have revealed no evidence of impaired fertility or harm to the fetus due to ciprofloxacin. In rabbits, ciprofloxacin (30 and 100 mg/kg orally) produced gastrointestinal disturbances resulting in maternal weight loss and an increased incidence of abortion. No teratogenicity was observed at either dose. After intravenous administration of doses up to 20 mg/kg, no maternal toxicity was produced, and no embryotoxicity or teratogenicity was observed. There are, however, no adequate and well-controlled studies in pregnant women. Ciprofloxacin should be used during pregnancy only if the potential benefit justifies the potential risk to the fetus. (See WARNINGS.)

Nursing Mothers: Ciprofloxacin is excreted in human milk. Because of the potential for serious adverse reactions in infants nursing from mothers taking ciprofloxacin, a decision should be made either to discontinue nursing or to discontinue the drug, taking into account the importance of the drug to the mother.

Pediatric Use: Safety and effectiveness in children and adolescents less than 18 years of age have not been established. Ciprofloxacin causes arthropathy in juvenile animals. (See WARNINGS.)

ADVERSE REACTIONS

During clinical investigation, 2,799 patients received 2,868 courses of the drug. Adverse events that were considered likely to be drug related occurred in 7.3% of courses, possibly related in 9.2%, (total of 16.5% thought to be possibly or probably related to drug therapy), and remotely related in 3.0%. Ciprofloxacin was discontinued because of an adverse event in 3.5% of courses, primarily involving the gastrointestinal system (1.5%), skin (0.6%), and central nervous system (0.4%). Those events typical of quinolones are italicized.

The most frequently reported events, drug related or not, were *nausea* (5.2%), *diarrhea* (2.3%), *vomiting* (2.0%), *abdominal pain/discomfort* (1.7%), *headache* (1.2%), *restlessness* (1.1%), and *rash* (1.1%).

Additional events that occurred in less than 1% of ciprofloxacin courses are listed below.

GASTROINTESTINAL: *(See above)*, painful oral mucosa, oral candidiasis, dysphagia, intestinal perforation, gastrointestinal bleeding.
CENTRAL NERVOUS SYSTEM: *(See above), dizziness, lightheadedness, insomnia, nightmares, hallucinations, manic reaction, irritability, tremor, ataxia, convulsive seizures, lethargy, drowsiness, weakness, malaise, anorexia, phobia, depersonalization, depression, paresthesia, toxic psychosis.*
SKIN/HYPERSENSITIVITY: *(See above), pruritus, urticaria, photosensitivity, flushing, fever, chills, angioedema, edema of the face, neck, lips, conjunctivae or hands;* cutaneous candidiasis, hyperpigmentation, erythema nodosum.

Allergic reactions ranging from urticaria to anaphylactic reactions have been reported (See WARNINGS).

SPECIAL SENSES: *blurred vision, disturbed vision (change in color perception, overbrightness of lights), decreased visual acuity, diplopia, eye pain, tinnitus, hearing loss, bad taste.*
MUSCULOSKELETAL: *joint or back pain, joint stiffness,* achiness, neck or chest pain, flare up of gout.
RENAL/UROGENITAL: *interstitial nephritis, nephritis, renal failure,* polyuria, urinary retention, urethral bleeding, vaginitis, acidosis.
CARDIOVASCULAR: palpitation, atrial flutter, ventricular ectopy, syncope, hypertension, angina pectoris, myocardial infarction, cardiopulmonary arrest, cerebral thrombosis.
RESPIRATORY: epistaxis, laryngeal or pulmonary edema, hiccough, hemoptysis, dyspnea, bronchospasm, pulmonary embolism.

Most of the adverse events reported were described as only mild or moderate in severity, abated soon after the drug was discontinued, and required no treatment.

In several instances nausea, vomiting, tremor, irritability or palpitation were judged by investigators to be related to elevated plasma levels of theophylline possibly as a result of drug interaction with ciprofloxacin.

Other adverse events reported in the postmarketing phase include anaphylactic reactions, erythema multiforme/Stevens-Johnson syndrome, exfoliative dermatitis, toxic epidermal necrolysis, vasculitis, jaundice, hepatic necrosis, postural hypotension, possible exacerbation of myasthenia gravis, anosmia, confusion, dysphasia, nystagmus, pseudomembranous colitis, pancreatitis, dyspepsia, flatulence, and constipation. Also reported were hemolytic anemia; agranulocytosis; elevation of serum triglycerides, serum cholesterol, blood glucose, serum potassium; prolongation of prothrombin time; albuminuria; candiduria, vaginal candidiasis; renal calculi, and change in serum phenytoin (See PRECAUTIONS).

Adverse Laboratory Changes: Changes in laboratory parameters listed as adverse events without regard to drug relationship:

Hepatic — Elevations of: ALT (SGPT) (1.9%), AST (SGOT) (1.7%), Alkaline Phosphatase (0.8%), LDH (0.4%), serum bilirubin (0.3%). Cholestatic jaundice has been reported.

Hematologic — Eosinophilia (0.6%), leukopenia (0.4%), decreased blood platelets (0.1%), elevated blood platelets (0.1%), pancytopenia (0.1%).

Renal — Elevations of: Serum creatinine (1.1%), BUN (0.9%). CRYSTALLURIA, CYLINDRURIA AND HEMATURIA HAVE BEEN REPORTED.

Other changes occurring in less than 0.1% of courses were: Elevation of serum gammaglutamyl transferase, elevation of serum amylase, reduction in blood glucose, elevated uric acid, decrease in hemoglobin, anemia, bleeding diathesis, increase in blood monocytes, leukocytosis.

OVERDOSAGE

In the event of acute overdosage the stomach should be emptied by inducing vomiting or by gastric lavage. The patient should be carefully observed and given supportive treatment. Adequate hydration must be maintained. Only a small amount of ciprofloxacin (<10%) is removed from the body after hemodialysis or peritoneal dialysis.

DOSAGE AND ADMINISTRATION

The usual adult dosage for patients with urinary tract infections is 250 mg every 12 hours. For patients with complicated infections caused by organisms not highly susceptible, 500 mg may be administered every 12 hours.

Lower respiratory tract infections, skin and skin structure infections, and bone and joint infections may be treated with 500 mg every 12 hours. For more severe or complicated infections, a dosage of 750 mg may be given every 12 hours.

The recommended dosage for Infectious Diarrhea is 500 mg every 12 hours.

DOSAGE GUIDELINES

Location of Infection	Type or Severity	Unit Dose	Frequency	Daily Dose
Urinary tract	Mild/Moderate	250 mg	q 12 h	500 mg
	Severe/Complicated	500 mg	q 12 h	1000 mg
Lower respiratory tract; Bone and Joint; Skin or Skin Structure	Mild/Moderate	500 mg	q 12 h	1000 mg
	Severe/Complicated	750 mg	q 12 h	1500 mg
Infectious Diarrhea	Mild/Moderate/Severe	500 mg	q 12 h	1000 mg

The determination of dosage for any particular patient must take into consideration the severity and nature of the infection, the susceptibility of the causative organism, the integrity of the patient's host-defense mechanisms, and the status of renal function.

The duration of treatment depends upon the severity of infection. Generally ciprofloxacin should be continued for at least 2 days after the signs and symptoms of infection have disappeared. The usual duration is 7 to 14 days; however, for severe and complicated infections more prolonged therapy may be required. Bone and joint infections may require treatment for 4 to 6 weeks or longer. Infectious Diarrhea may be treated for 5-7 days.

Impaired Renal Function: Ciprofloxacin is eliminated primarily by renal excretion; however, the drug is also metabolized and partially cleared through the biliary system of the liver and through the intestine. These alternate pathways of drug elimination appear to compensate for the reduced renal excretion in patients with renal impairment. Nonetheless, some modification of dosage is recommended, particularly for patients with severe renal dysfunction. The following table provides dosage guidelines for use in patients with renal impairment; however, monitoring of serum drug levels provides the most reliable basis for dosage adjustment:

RECOMMENDED STARTING AND MAINTENANCE DOSES FOR PATIENTS WITH IMPAIRED RENAL FUNCTION

Creatinine Clearance (mL/min)	Dose
> 50	See Usual Dosage
30 – 50	250 – 500 mg q 12 h
5 – 29	250 – 500 mg q 18 h
Patients on hemodialysis or Peritoneal dialysis	250 – 500 mg q 24 h (after dialysis)

When only the serum creatinine concentration is known, the following formula may be used to estimate creatinine clearance.

$$\text{Men: Creatinine clearance (mL/min)} = \frac{\text{Weight (kg)} \times (140 - \text{age})}{72 \times \text{serum creatinine (mg/dL)}}$$

Women: $0.85 \times$ the value calculated for men.

The serum creatinine should represent a steady state of renal function.

In patients with severe infections and severe renal impairment, a unit dose of 750 mg may be administered at the intervals noted above; however, patients should be carefully monitored and the serum ciprofloxacin concentration should be measured periodically. Peak concentrations (1-2 hours after dosing) should generally range from 2 to 4 mcg/mL.

For patients with changing renal function or for patients with renal impairment and hepatic insufficiency, measurement of serum concentrations of ciprofloxacin will provide additional guidance for adjusting dosage.

HOW SUPPLIED

Cipro® (ciprofloxacin hydrochloride) is available as round, slightly yellowish film-coated tablets containing 250 mg ciprofloxacin. The 250-mg tablet is coded with the word "Miles" on one side and "512" on the reverse side. Cipro® is also available as capsule shaped, slightly yellowish film-coated tablets containing 500 mg or 750 mg ciprofloxacin. The 500-mg tablet is coded with the word "Miles" on one side and "513" on the reverse side; the 750-mg tablet is coded with the word "Miles" on one side and "514" on the reverse side. Available in bottles of 50's, 100's and in Unit Dose packages of 100.

	Strength	NDC Code	Tablet Identification
Bottles of 50:	750 mg	NDC 0026-8514-50	Miles 514
Bottles of 100:	250 mg	NDC 0026-8512-51	Miles 512
	500 mg	NDC 0026-8513-51	Miles 513
Unit Dose Package of 100:	250 mg	NDC 0026-8512-48	Miles 512
	500 mg	NDC 0026-8513-48	Miles 513
	750 mg	NDC 0026-8514-48	Miles 514

Store below 86°F (30°C).

ANIMAL PHARMACOLOGY

Ciprofloxacin and related drugs have been shown to cause arthropathy in immature animals of most species tested (See WARNINGS). Damage of weight bearing joints was observed in juvenile dogs and rats. In young beagles 100 mg/kg ciprofloxacin given daily for 4 weeks, caused degenerative articular changes of the knee joint. At 30 mg/kg the effect on the joint was minimal. In a subsequent study in beagles removal of weight bearing from the joint reduced the lesions but did not totally prevent them.

Crystalluria, sometimes associated with secondary nephropathy, occurs in laboratory animals dosed with ciprofloxacin. This is primarily related to the reduced solubility of ciprofloxacin under alkaline conditions, which predominate in the urine of test animals; in man, crystalluria is rare since human urine is typically acidic. In rhesus monkeys, crystalluria without nephropathy has been noted after single oral doses as low as 5 mg/kg. After 6 months of intravenous dosing at 10 mg/kg/day, no nephropathological changes were noted; however, nephropathy was observed after dosing at 20 mg/kg/day for the same duration.

In dogs, ciprofloxacin at 3 and 10 mg/kg by rapid IV injection (15 sec.) produces pronounced hypotensive effects. These effects are considered to be related to histamine release since they are partially antagonized by pyrilamine, an antihistamine. In rhesus monkeys, rapid IV injection also produces hypotension but the effect in this species is inconsistent and less pronounced.

In mice, concomitant administration of nonsteroidal anti-inflammatory drugs such as fenbufen, phenylbutazone and indomethacin, with quinolones has been reported to enhance the CNS stimulatory effect of quinolones.

Ocular toxicity seen with some related drugs has not been observed in ciprofloxacin-treated animals.

References: 1. Barry AL, Jones RN, Thornsberry C, et al. Antibacterial activities of ciprofloxacin, norfloxacin, oxolinic acid, cinoxacin, and nalidixic acid. *Antimicrob Agents Chemother.* 1984;25:633-637. **2.** Guimaraes MA, Noone P. The comparative in-vitro activity of norfloxacin, ciprofloxacin, enoxacin and nalidixic acid against 423 strains of gram-negative rods and staphylococci isolated from infected hospitalised patients. *J Antimicrob Chemother.* 1986;17:63-67. **3.** Van Caekenberghe DL, Pattyn SR. In vitro activity of ciprofloxacin compared with those of other new fluorinated piperazinyl-substituted quinoline derivatives. *Antimicrob Agents Chemother.* 1984;25:518-521.

COMMITTED TO THERAPEUTIC EFFICIENCY

Miles Inc.
Pharmaceutical Division
400 Morgan Lane
West Haven, CT 06516

Caution: Federal (USA) Law prohibits dispensing without a prescription.

PZ100735   8/91   Bay o 9867   5202-2-A-U.S.-3   1577
© 1991 Miles Inc.   Printed in USA